Because Water Is Life is a supple, specific, and critically engaging book that will be profoundly useful to teachers and students. Gary Chamberlain hones his analytic, constructive insights into a text that is utterly invaluable for all conversations about water and Catholic social teaching. I recommend this gripping and accessible book to everyone who seeks to understand further the legacy of CST and how that tradition offers pathways toward water ethics.

—Christiana Zenner
Fordham University

Chamberlain's book about water as life, as common good, and as sacrament for the whole world should wake us to greater care for our Earth and its water both as our home and a gift from God.

—David Leigh, SJ
Seattle University

Gary Chamberlain brings the vital and energizing moral teachings of the Catholic Church to bear on the crises of pollution, hoarding, and overconsumption threatening our planet's fresh waters. This book develops an original, accessible, and crucial argument relevant to anyone interested in Catholic social teaching, water, and environmental ethics. *Because Water Is Life* is an excellent and inspiring resource for classrooms, churches, and anyone who wants to think with religious tradition about how to build a better future on Earth.

—Kevin J. O'Brien
Pacific Lutheran University

Author Acknowledgments

This work owes much to the teaching and research into two of my favorite topics, the global water crises and Catholic social teaching. My great thanks for the invitation from the editors at Anselm Academic, Brad Harmon and Maura Hagarty, to put together these two areas in *Because Water Is Life*. Brad has since moved on, but I owe Maura a great deal for her continuing guidance and patience as the work moved forward. She has been stalwart in her suggestions and support.

I also want to express my thanks to the three Anselm Academic editors who reviewed the text and offered very helpful comments and suggestions for improvement, Beth Erickson, Annie Belt, and Kate Matracia.

My thanks especially to my colleagues Christiana Zenner, associate professor of theology, Fordham University, and Kevin O'Brien, associate professor of Christian ethics, Pacific Lutheran University, for their encouragement and work on water and climate change. A special thanks to colleague Phil Thompson, professor of civil and environmental engineering, Seattle University, and currently Director of the Center for Environmental Justice and Sustainability, for his own research and work on practical applications of technology, leading students to work on water issues in countries around the world. Finally, special thanks to June Bube Johnson, associate professor of English, Seattle University, who has involved her students in global issues, such as water and sanitation, and to Gordon Miller, adjunct professor of environmental studies and former Director of the Environmental Studies Program, for his encouragement and support over several years of my environmental studies course involving water issues and religion.

My thanks to Fr. Pat Howell, SJ, friend who encouraged me and offered fine advice; to Fr. Peter Henriot, SJ, long-time friend and advocate for environmental and social justice, until recently stationed in Zambia and Malawi; and to Fr. Dave Leigh, SJ, who worked with me on seminars on Catholic social teaching over many summers; Dave still carries on that important work.

Thanks too to Paul Peterhans, educator and source of many materials on the environment, and to former students Erin Duncan and Danica Hendrickson, who continually inform me of important concerns around water and environmental justice.

And finally I want to thank my family: my wife, Sharon; sons, Benjamin and Michael; and daughter-in-law, Beth, for their reviews of particular chapters and important advice about readership.

Publisher Acknowledgments

Thank you to the following individuals who reviewed this work in progress:

Kevin Ahern, *Manhattan College, Riverdale, New York*
John Hart, *Boston University, Boston, Massachusetts*
Jennifer Reed-Bouley, *College of Saint Mary, Omaha, Nebraska*

BECAUSE WATER IS LIFE

CATHOLIC SOCIAL TEACHING CONFRONTS EARTH'S WATER CRISES

GARY L. CHAMBERLAIN

ANSELM
ACADEMIC

Dedication

Dedicated to grandson Nicholas Lawrence Chamberlain,
born February 5, 2017, in the midst of this writing . . .
and to all future water protectors.

And to dear friend Bill Fuchs, scientist, environmental
and justice advocate, who died all too young at forty-one.

Created by the publishing team of Anselm Academic.

The Scriptural quotations in this book are from *The Jerusalem Bible*, Garden City, NY: Doubleday, 1966.

Cover image: © mycteria / shutterstock.com

Printed in the United States of America

7086

ISBN 978-1-59982-914-2

Contents

Introduction

In *The Rime of the Ancient Mariner*, with its theme of sin and redemption, nineteenth-century poet Samuel Coleridge writes, "Water, water everywhere / And all the boards did shrink. / Water, water everywhere, / Nor any drop to drink."[1]

These words carry significant weight when we consider that nondrinkable, nonpotable saltwater comprises 97 percent of all water on Earth. But then, consider the words of this early twentieth-century ballad: "All day I've faced the barren waste / without the taste of water, cool water."[2]

These literary examples compare and contrast the ocean and desert—one with abundant but deadly seawater and the other with its absence of drinking water. A study of water in today's world reveals a series of frightening, human-caused crises: Arctic ice melting at rapid rates, seawater too acidic for coral reefs and shellfish, wetlands drained for development, water polluted by agricultural runoff and mining waste, new dams that displace millions of people, rivers running dry. These examples are not natural disasters; they are disasters caused by human policies and practices.

Water remains our most precious resource, key to life on Earth and survival for all. Yet, because there seems to be an abundance of water, we may wonder, "What is the problem?" Consider that 97 percent of Earth's water belongs to oceans; of the 3 percent remaining, ice and permafrost take up 2 percent, which leaves only 1 percent for humans, other living beings, and Earth itself.

The importance of addressing the world's water crises cannot be underestimated, and Catholic social teaching (CST) provides an excellent tool for ethical analyses of questions about the use and abuse of water.

---

1. Samuel Taylor Coleridge, *The Rime of the Ancient Mariner*, in *The Norton Anthology of English Literature*, Vol. II, 6th ed., ed. M. H. Abrams (New York: W. W. Norton, 1993), 296.

2. Lyrics by Bob Nolan, 1936, recorded by Sons of the Pioneers, available on the LetsSingIt website.

Distribution of Earth's Water[3]

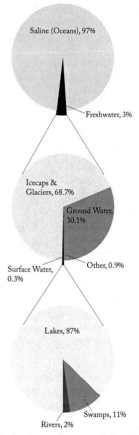

Saline (Oceans), 97%

Freshwater, 3%

Icecaps & Glaciers, 68.7%

Ground Water, 30.1%

Surface Water, 0.3%

Other, 0.9%

Lakes, 87%

Swamps, 11%

Rivers, 2%

Only three percent of Earth's water is fresh (see top pie chart). The middle pie chart shows how freshwater is distributed, and the bottom chart shows how Earth's fresh surface water is distributed.

Although there are many understandings of ethics, Catholic theologian Dan Maguire sees ethics as "the art/science that seeks to bring sensitivity and method to the discernment of moral values."[4] As humans and other life face challenges with water supply, a new water ethic is needed, and CST can foster that.

Let us begin, for example, with a snapshot of water events in 2016.

Earth Day

On Earth Day, April 22, 2016, in Paris world leaders signed a historic agreement on climate change, pledging to undertake serious efforts to halt or reverse a rise in global average temperature that among other things impacts salt, fresh, and frozen water worldwide.[5] Meanwhile, in New York City, a unique mix of monks, nuns, students, and other citizens gathered for the annual Blessing of the Gowanus River. Widely considered the country's dirtiest waterway and "the most toxic spot in New York City," the 1.8-mile canal holds sludge accumulated from years of discharges from the city. Fr. Patrick Boyle, a Catholic priest, entreated those gathered on

3. The data presented in this diagram is from US Geological Survey. See Victor Ponce, "Groundwater Utilization and Sustainability," at *groundwater.sdsu.edu.*

4. Daniel C. Maguire and A. Nicholas Fargnoli, *On Moral Grounds: The Art/Science of Ethics* (New York: Crossroad, 1991), 34.

5. Justin Gillis and Coral Davenport, "Leaders Meet to Sign a Climate Pact Fraught with Uncertainties," *New York Times*, April 22, 2016, A12. President Donald Trump has stated that the United States will pull out of the agreement, a process that will take four years.

Earth Day to join him "to invoke God's blessings upon the waters of the Gowanus Canal." He figured blessing the canal was as good an idea as any to solve a hundred years' worth of toxic sludge. Those gathered thought, "Can it hurt to pray? Who knows what can happen?"[6]

Also on Earth Day 2016, in Flint, Michigan, three officials were indicted for negligence and tampering with evidence in the investigation into the lead in the city's drinking water.[7] The Flint story began back in April 2014, when the city switched its water supply from the city of Detroit to the Flint River; the city was facing bankruptcy, and the switch cut costs. Despite local, state, and even national assurances that Flint's drinking water was safe, the citizens of Flint immediately noticed their water now had an unusual color, bitter taste, and foul odor. The Flint story is a vivid illustration of the human and environmental injustice resulting from misuse and abuse of this precious, natural resource.

A gift from the Creator for the benefit of Earth and all living things, water and its human use and abuse is at the heart of today's environmental crises. Ethical analyses, such as those found in CST, challenge the environmental and social injustices involved and call for corrective action.

Let us start by looking at the range of water crises worldwide.

Water Crises Worldwide

According to a 2015 United Nations report, 783 million people lack access to clean water.[8] The statistics which result from that fact are grim:

- Sub-Saharan Africa is among the regions with the greatest drinking-water spending needs, with the greatest investment needs in rural areas.
- One in nine people worldwide does not have access to safe and clean drinking water.
- About 443 million school days are lost each year due to water-related diseases.

---

6. Corey Kilgannon, "Invoking a Higher Power to Clean up the Gowanus Canal," *New York Times*, April 22, 2016, A16.

7. William Schutte, "Seeking Justice for Flint Residents," *New York Times*, April 22, 2016, A24.

8. "Water," United Nations, *www.un.org/en/sections/issues-depth/water/*.

- In developing countries, as much as 80 percent of illnesses are linked to poor water and sanitation conditions.
- Exposure to unsafe drinking water, inadequate sanitation, and poor hygiene is a leading cause of cholera and a variety of infectious and tropical diseases in the African region.
- Half of the world's hospital beds are filled with people suffering from a water-related disease.
- Girls under the age of fifteen are twice as likely as boys to be the family member responsible for fetching water.
- More than half of the developing world's primary schools don't have access to water and sanitation facilities. Without toilets, girls often drop out at puberty.[9]

Ocean Acidification

Meanwhile, ocean waters are growing more acidic due to human practices that release unhealthy levels of carbon dioxide into the atmosphere; some of this excess carbon reacts with water molecules, causing ocean acidification. (High levels of carbon dioxide released daily into Earth's atmosphere are also a key cause of climate change.) Ocean acidification and rising global temperatures, in turn, are causing the die-off of coral reefs, which are central to the survival of many marine species.[10] In addition, globally, there are 408 oceanic "dead zones," that is, areas with no or low oxygen and hence little or no life. Dead zones occur when polluted water from agricultural runoff, plant expulsions into surrounding waterways, landscape runoff and other sources pour into surrounding rivers. The largest dead zone in US waters is in the Gulf of Mexico near the mouth of the Mississippi.[11] Cruise ships produce some 30,000 gallons of sewage and 19 tons of garbage daily, which are mostly dumped at sea.[12] Every year, 3.5 million tons of oil is spilled into the world's oceans.[13]

9. "Facts about Water: Statistics of the Water Crisis," *https://thewaterproject.org/water-scarcity/water_stats*, updated August 31, 2016.

10. Juliet Eliperin, "Growing Acidity of Oceans May Kill Corals," *Washington Post*, July 5, 2006, A1.

11. John Nielsen, "'Dead Zones' Multiplying in World's Oceans," *Morning Edition*, National Public Radio, August 15, 2008.

12. Jonathan Stein, "Enemies of the Ocean," *Mother Jones* (March/April 2006), 50.

13. Philip Ball, *Life's Matrix: A Biography of Water* (New York: Farrar, Straus and Giroux, 1999), 354.

All of these water crises stem from human practices. This is both good news and bad news. If people, governments, and international agencies act now to stop or improve these practices, the environmental and social damage now underway can be stopped or even reversed. Achieving either of these, however, involves not only educating people but also making deep structural and behavioral changes. What is happening to water is the cost of human consumptive practices driven by public policies that benefit a few at the expense of most of the world's people and species.

Water Scarcity

In addition, due to population growth and the increasing demand for fresh, drinkable water, six billion people could face water scarcity by 2050. The world's population is expected to grow another 50 percent by 2050, with large numbers moving to urban areas.[14] In megacities of more than ten million people, residents use more water than rural dwellers, because they consume more meat, thus placing huge burdens on water.

In addition, here are some samples of water consumed in manufacturing or producing a variety of products for consumption:

- Bread, 1 pound = about 200 gallons
- Chicken, 1 pound = 500 gallons per pound
- Coffee, 1 cup = 35 gallons
- Ground beef, ¼ pound = 460 gallons
- One cotton shirt = 650 gallons
- Chocolate 2.2 pounds = 4 gallons
- Pork, 1 pound = 790 gallons[15]

Effects of Global Warming

Water is also affected by human-caused global warming, which intensifies the hydrologic cycle. "A warmer atmosphere holds more

14. Michael Specter, "The Last Drop: Confronting the Possibility of a Global Catastrophe," *New Yorker*, October 23, 2006, *www.newyorker.com/magazine/2006/10/23/the-last-drop-2*.

15. "The Water Content of Things," US Geological Survey, 2016, *https://water.usgs.gov/edu/activity-watercontent.html*; "How Much Water Is Needed to Produce Food and How Much Do We Waste?" 2016, *www.theguardian.com/news/datablog/2013/jan/10/how-much-water-food-production-waste*. The amounts include water for growing, cleaning, producing, etc.

water, and increasing cloudiness reduces daytime warming and retards nighttime cooling by blocking outgoing long-wave radiation." This results in heavier rainfalls, more flash flooding, a northward drift of semitropical plants and animals, and other problems. Consensus "is building that the temperature increases resulting from a doubling of atmospheric carbon dioxide will change the world's basic hydrologic cycle by increasing both evaporation and precipitation," from 7 to 15 percent.[16] These are but a few of the world's water-related crises; many more remain.

Fracking

Of more recent concern is hydraulic fracturing, or fracking, in which a well is drilled to find oil and gas deposits deep in the earth. Once located, a soup of millions of gallons of water, sand, and chemicals is pumped into the well under extremely high pressure to fracture shale and bring the oil or gas to the surface. Along with the oil or gas comes a combination of briny waste, "10 times saltier than sea water."[17] The chemicals used in fracking and the surface pools of waste that result severely damage human and animal skin, eyes, and sensory organs; throats, stomachs, intestines, and livers; brain and nervous systems; and immune systems.[18]

In sum, Earth's waters are suffering—from climate change; human overpopulation, and increasing overconsumption; daily pollution; water waste in ever-increasing agricultural, industrial, and personal human use; lake, river, and groundwater diversions; and hydraulic fracturing. Water is a precious natural resource. Water is renewable—a gift in the frame of religious traditions—but finite. Human consumptive practices have cut the amount of fresh, clean water as human demand is rising. Truly, there is not "a drop to drink" of "water, cool water"—for all too many of Earth's people and creatures, and for Earth itself.

---

16. Marq de Villiers, *Water: The Fate of Our Most Precious Resource* (New York: Houghton-Mifflin, 2000), 80.

17. Abraham Lustgarten, "Hydrofracked: One Man's Quest for Answers about Natural Gas Drilling," *High Country News,* June 27, 2011, 11, 20.

18. For a fruitful discussion, see David Freeman and Timothy Gower, "Big Gulp," *Reader's Digest* (August, 2011): 103; and Christiana Z. Peppard, *Just Water: Theology, Ethics, and the Global Water Crisis* (Maryknoll, NY: Orbis Books, 2014), 142–70.

A Finite Resource

The problem with water, writes Marq de Villiers, winner of the prestigious Canadian Governor General Literary Award for his work on water, is that there is no more than what we have, but there are more people coming. "And all those people are utterly dependent on water for their lives, for their livelihoods, their food, and, increasingly, their industry." We consume water and waste it with little attention to the consequences. The result, decries de Villiers, is "the human population is burgeoning, but water demand is increasing twice as fast."[19]

Why Catholic Social Teaching?

As a student at Saint Louis University, I discovered CST almost by accident. I was so moved by the power of these writings that I naively thought, "If only people, or at least Catholics, read these writings, we could change the world." However, I quickly learned that most people did not read these documents, and a long and dense abstract document does not move most people to action. These realities dashed my hopes and crushed my idealism. Yet that thought persisted, and I carried it into my years teaching high school seniors by incorporating CST into my classes. I doubt my students held the same enthusiasm for these writings as I, but at least they heard them.

After finishing graduate studies, I moved to Seattle in 1979. There, in this city by the sea, at Seattle University, I again taught courses incorporating CST, which my friend and colleague, Peter Henriot, SJ, called "our best-kept secret." Many of the students were not Christian or Catholic, and many Catholic students who knew of Roman Catholic teachings only through the Catholic Church's teachings on sexuality perceived them as out of date or irrelevant to their lives. Thus, students often resented being taught anything "Catholic" and were puzzled about how the Church's teachings could possibly embrace social justice, concern for the environment, peace, and human rights. By the

---

19. De Villiers, *Water*, 12–13.

end of our time together, however, many developed an appreciation of CST and how its principles applied to diverse current issues.

Today, CST can be applied to the world's water crises. These crises require a new water ethic, a fundamentally different approach to how humans understand and value water. "The essence of such an ethic is to make the protection of freshwater ecosystems a central goal in all that we do,"[20] writes Sandra Postel, Director of the Global Water Project and expert on freshwater issues and related ecosystems.

CST offers a specific, concrete approach to the ethical analysis needed in future discussions of water, water access and management, and the human right to water. This book focuses on the principles in CST as they apply to water. So fundamental is this precious resource to human physical and spiritual realms that humans take it for granted even as they cannot live without it.

What Is Catholic Social Teaching?

Catholic social teaching has developed throughout the history of the Roman Catholic Church. CST is rooted in the Jewish and Christian Scriptures and Christian thought from the early church to the present times. It is drawn from biblical accounts, especially the Jewish prophets and the life of Jesus, through writers during the early church's emergence in the Roman Empire, the medieval period, and present times. However, the term *Catholic social teaching* has come to primarily refer to a collection of writings and actions from 1891 to the present.[21] In view of the limits of space, the focus in this

---

20. Sandra Postel, "The Missing Piece: A Water Ethic," in *Water Ethics: Foundational Readings for Students and Professionals*, ed. Peter G. Brown and Jeremy J. Schmidt (Washington, DC: Island Press, 2010), 221–25.

21. For excellent discussions of the biblical roots of CST, see John Donoghue, "Biblical Perspectives on Justice," in *The Faith That Does Justice*, ed. John C. Haughey (New York: Paulist Press, 1977), 68–112; also John Donoghue, "The Bible and Catholic Social Teaching," in *Modern Catholic Social Teaching*, ed. Kenneth Himes (Washington, DC: Georgetown University Press, 2004), 9–40; and Mary Katherine Birge, SSJ, "Biblical Justice," in *The Heart of Catholic Social Teaching*, ed. David M. McCarty (Grand Rapids, MI: Brazos Press, 2009), 19–30. Also relevant is the *Compendium of the Social Doctrine of the Church*, Pontifical Council for Justice and Peace (PCJP) (Washington, DC: US Conference of Catholic Bishops [USCCB], 2011), 115–19, among other sections.

discussion will be on what is called "Catholic social teaching" from the period of the "social question" in the late 1890s in Europe—that is, how does the church respond to the increasingly secular forces in the modern liberal state and the plight of workers—to the present time, with emerging concerns about the environment. Although there are many sources from the late 1890s to the present day (statements of local and regional bishops, religious communities of priests and nuns, national Catholic organizations, and powerful personal voices in the tradition), the emphasis will be on the specific documents published by the Vatican under the authorship of the popes at the time.

CST principles address developments in a particular context, time, and place and then expand to address events in a new context, time, and place. For example, in 1891 at the height of the Industrial Revolution, Pope Leo XIII's encyclical *Rerum novarum* (*On the Condition of Labor*) was a groundbreaking attempt to address the situation of impoverished and overworked workers in Europe and the United States. In 2015, Pope Francis, in *Laudato si': Praise Be to You*, with the subtitle *On Care for Our Common Home*, undertakes a critical examination of the environmental crises around climate change, water, and human consumption. CST responds to the social, economic, political, and now environmental realities of the times.

Two objections to CST frequently arise: 1) Why call the teachings "Catholic"? and 2) How can popes, bishops, and Catholic laypeople write about political, economic, and social realities when they have no academic expertise in those areas? First, the teachings are "Catholic" in that they emerge from the history of the Church—from its scripture and traditions, with their roots in small, often persecuted communities. CST writers comment on the evils surrounding wealth and poverty in these communities, and the Church's founding of hospitals, orphanages, and houses of refuge and hospitality throughout the centuries is testimony to the relevance of these teachings. Yet CST also concerns the philosophical history of natural law, adopted and adapted from Greek and Roman thought, and the theological emphasis from scripture and philosophical sources upon the dignity of persons and communities in relation to the Creator. Finally, CST reflects upon contemporary social and natural sciences and the experiences of churches and other communities around the globe, especially in documents from 1891 to present.

Second, some feel that bishops and popes—not being experts in economics or politics—are overstepping their limits and should stick to Church and spiritual matters. This response sometimes comes from Catholics who are challenged by the teachings. For example, William Buckley, a leading Catholic conservative writer and founder of *The National Review*, famously retorted to Pope John XXIII's 1961 encyclical *Mater et magistra* (*Christianity and Social Progress*), "*Mater si, Magistra no!*" (Mother, yes; teacher, no!). Buckley and others forget that although these documents are written in the name of popes and bishops, the popes and bishops rely heavily upon experts in the fields of politics, economics, social science, and contemporary science. More fundamentally, Church leaders are concerned about all people and where there are injustice, discrimination, unfair accumulation of wealth, and harm to the environment—in these cases, Church leaders have come to see their role and obligation to challenge the existing structures perpetuating these problems.[22]

In the *Compendium of the Social Doctrine of the Church*, the Vatican's Pontifical Council for Justice and Peace (PCJP) states:

"The Church has the right to be a teacher for mankind [*sic*], a teacher of the truth of faith: the truth not only of dogmas but also of the morals. . . . Because of the public relevance of the Gospel and faith, because of the corrupting effects of injustice, that is, of sin, the Church cannot remain indifferent to social matters."[23]

Catholic Social Teaching: "Our Best-kept Secret"

If Church documents have such authority, why are they seldom read by Catholics and others? Why are they called our best-kept secret?[24] There are several reasons. A major problem with the documents lies

---

22. There have been many other sources for CST throughout the centuries, including national and regional organizations, particular people who incorporate these teachings, various documents written before 1891, and so forth. For this book, I examine the documents released by the Vatican and some national bishops' conferences from 1891 to present.

23. Pontifical Council for Justice and Peace, *Compendium of the Social Doctrine of the Church* (Washington, DC: US Conference of Catholic Bishops [USCCB], 2011).

24. Peter Henriot, SJ, et al., *Catholic Social Teaching: Our Best Kept Secret* (Maryknoll, NY: Orbis Books, 2003).

in their tone, or readability. With one or two notable exceptions,[25] the texts are long and highly academic. When laypeople try to read them, they "often walk away more confused than when they began."[26]

Another issue is that the Church does not do a good job of communicating CST. When writing the 1971 document *Justice in the World*, the international assembly of bishops gathered in Rome asked why it was that although many knew the Church teachings on sexuality quite well, they remained—after eighty years—largely unaware of the Church's social teachings.[27] In 1998, US Catholic bishops released a study of 113 Catholic institutions of higher education, titled *Sharing Catholic Social Teachings*. "While there is clear interest in and support for Catholic social teaching," they wrote, "it is generally not offered in a systematic way. There appears to be little consistent attention given to incorporating Catholic social teaching into general education courses."[28] Last, while CST is the official teaching of the Church, these writings relate to specific issues at particular times, issues about which there can be reasonable disagreement. Teachers, lay leaders, and others who might pass on the great tradition of CST need to devote significant time unearthing a document's context. There are disagreements over specific translations, because the documents are written in Latin, and translations often miss the full power of a principle or argument. Using the issue of worldwide water crises, this book aims to address such problems and show how CST applies to a specific current issue.

Method

Chapter 1, "The Rise of Catholic Social Teaching," provides a historical overview of the major CST teachings. Each section focuses on a particular document's emerging principles around issues of the day, followed by examples, in some cases, of the implications and

---

25. One example of a very different, vibrant approach is the 1975 pastoral letter "This Land Is Home to Me," written as a poem by the bishops of Appalachia.

26. Jozef Zalot and Benedict Guevin, *Catholic Ethics in Today's World* (Anselm Academic: Winona, MN, 2011), 1.

27. Thomas Gumbleton, "Peacemaking as a Way of Life," in *One Hundred Years of Catholic Social Thought*, ed. John Coleman (Maryknoll, NY: Orbis Books, 1991), 306.

28. US Catholic Conference, "Sharing Catholic Social Teaching: Challenges and Directions" (Washington, DC: US Catholic Conference, 1998), 8–9.

applications of those principles in the life of the Church and among people who apply these principles in their lives and in social and political policies. The chief focus will be on how these principles can be used in the analyses of global water crises.

Following chapters examine relevant principles in relation to a specific water issue. Chapter 2, "Climate Change as Structural Violence," explores climate change and the CST principles of the common good, the universal destination of the goods of creation, the preferential option for the poor, and participation in decision making as a dimension of human dignity.

Chapter 3, "A Polluted Earth in the Twenty-first Century," examines water pollution with the particular case of water pollution in Flint, Michigan. The analysis employs CST principles concerning poverty, human dignity, racism, and social justice in decision making. Then, considering the scarcity of water for many and the abundance for a few, chapter 4, "Water Scarcity for Most and Abundance for Few," applies CST principles such as the common good of the community, equity for all, and the right of participation in local decisions. Chapter 5, "Extraction from the Earth: Impacts of Mining and Fracking on Water and People," covers water use in resource extraction and hydraulic fracturing to show the CST demand for local voices, especially the voices of the poor, along with the principle of the care of creation. Chapter 6, "Selling Water: Privatization of a Scarce Resource," takes up the corporate privatization of water and, in particular, the use of bottled water in relation to CST principles of human rights, uses of public goods like water, and issues surrounding cultural integrity and indigenous peoples. Chapter 7, "The Right to Water," examines the basis for declaring water a human right, a right essential to human dignity.

Chapter 8, "A New Water Ethic: Because Water Is Life," takes up the thorny question of where to go from here. This chapter examines some new technological approaches to the world's water crises. More fundamental questions about water's place in humanity's understanding of its interaction with Earth must also be asked. A section of this final chapter is devoted to the Catholic Church's public worship practices and rituals, to the dynamics of a creation-centered theological approach to Earth, and to an examination of the spirituality of water. These reflections call for new ethical and theological reflections on CST as part of the call for a new water ethic.

CHAPTER

The Rise of Catholic Social Teaching

The history of Catholic social teaching (CST) is complex, in large part because each document has emerged from the context of a particular time, place, and series of events. This chapter introduces Church social teachings that explore principles or themes which form the ethical framework for the analysis of global water crises.

Thematic Movements in Catholic Social Teaching

There is a dynamic movement in CST—from concerns about justice for workers in *Rerum novarum* (*On the Condition of Labor*) of 1891 to concerns about justice for Earth in *Laudato si': On Care for Our Common Home* of 2015. The meaning of justice that best fits this discussion comes from biblical scholar John Donoghue, who described justice as "fidelity to the demands of a relationship."[1] This meaning fits well with the notion of human rights, or demands, made on the basis of relationships with others, communities, God, and Earth. The key to those relationships is faithfulness and fidelity. Exploration of these relationships lies at the heart of this chapter. Relationships considered in CST include those between labor and capital in 1891; workers, management, and owners in 1931; and states and groups

---

1. Donoghue, "Biblical Perspectives on Justice," 69.

within societies from the 1960s through the 1980s and with the natural environment from the 1990s to recent years. Rather than starting in 1891, with Leo XIII's *Rerum novarum* (literally "Of the New Things"), this discussion will begin with Pope Francis's 2015 encyclical *Laudato si'*.[2] This encyclical addresses the current realities facing Earth as "our common home," water, ecology, and culture.

Pope Francis and *Laudato si'*

On March 13, 2013, Cardinal Jorge Mario Bergoglio from Argentina was elected pope, the first Latin American and first Jesuit to become pope. He took the name of Francis in honor of Francis of Assisi, late twelfth-century Franciscan friar, who was, he says, "particularly concerned for God's creation and for the poor and outcast,"[3] as well as the connection between harm to the environment and harm to people.

Laudato si' opens with a strong reference to the intimate relations of humans with Earth: "our common home is like a sister with whom we share our life and a beautiful mother who opens her arms to embrace us." But this sister/mother is suffering. "This sister now cries out to us because of the harm we have inflicted on her by our irresponsible use and abuse of the goods with which God has endowed her" (*LS* 1, 2, 160).

Francis focuses on humanity's relationship to Earth, not in abstract terms, but in a more intimate manner, recalling that we humans are ourselves "the dust of the ground" (Gen 2:7) and live in a shared "home." For Francis, Earth—like people, and the poor in particular—is mistreated, suffering, abused by pollution and climate change, and filled with tainted water, unfit for consumption.

---

2. For a fine overview of CST in relation to the context, peoples, and groups involved, see Marvin L. Krier Mich, *Catholic Social Teaching and Movements* (Mystic, CT: Twenty-Third Publications, 1998); and John Coleman, ed., *One Hundred Years of Catholic Social Thought* (Maryknoll, NY: Orbis Books, 1991), among others.

3. Pope Francis, *Laudato si': On Care for Our Common Home*, encyclical letter, 2015, *http://w2.vatican.va/content/francisco/en/encyclicals/documents/papa-francisco_20150524_enciclica-laudato-si.html*. Copyright © Libreria Editrice Vaticana (LEV). Used by permission.

First, Francis examines threats to "our common home" (*LS* 17–61),[4] two of which relate to the themes of this book: climate change and water (*LS* 24–25). He devotes an entire section to water issues (*LS* 27–31), outlining problems involving water scarcity, pollution, waste, and the troubling movement toward privatization (*LS* 48). Later in his encyclical, Francis states unequivocally that the right to water is fundamental to the dignity of persons, the common good, and the exercise of other human rights (*LS* 30, 185).

Francis sees God's imprint in the least element of creation, whether a leaf or a human. All are interconnected as aspects of the divine spirit (*LS* 74–92). "The ideal is . . . to discover God in all things" (*LS* 233). Thus, Earth, habitat of all, is for a collective good, not something for one group to exploit, but a universal gift with its own integrity and dwelling of the Divine (*LS* 93–95).

Francis links what other popes called "integral development"[5] with environmental integrity and introduces the phrase "integral ecology"[6] (*LS* 137ff). "Everything is closely related" (*LS* 137), he says. Threats that lead to environmental degradation can also undo social structures and harm, or even cause the disappearance of, cultures (*LS* 144). The pope calls for special care of indigenous peoples, their histories, and their places on Earth. Here is a new emphasis upon indigenous peoples, severely impacted by the diminishment of water and other demands of economic development (*LS* 137, 143ff).

Finally, Francis calls for a new ecological awareness to penetrate our choices about consumption of Earth's resources, an awareness that includes a sense of environmental justice, intergenerational justice toward future generations, and especially, justice for the poor (*LS* 147). This process includes new forms of education and a new "ecological spirituality" that "can motivate us to a more passionate concern for the protection of our world" (*LS* 209ff, 216, 228).

---

4. Several areas are discussed: pollution and climate change; water, loss of biodiversity, decline in the quality of human life, global inequality weak responses, and a variety of opinions.

5. ". . . the development of each man and of the whole man," Pope Paul VI, *Populorum progressio*, 14.

6. The term describes human and Earth integrity or wholeness. It will be developed more fully in later chapters.

Impacts of *Laudato si'*

Here are just a few of the many examples of the impact of Francis's encyclical. On the second anniversary of the encyclical, Cardinal Luis Tagle, Archbishop of Manila, Philippines, asked Catholics to take a pledge to "pray for and with creation, live more simply and advocate to protect our common home."[7] Joan Brown, executive director of New Mexico Interfaith Power and Light, recently stressed the importance of Francis's encyclical in framing climate change as a moral concern, not merely an economic or technological one. And in May 2017, nine US Catholic organizations announced their plans to divest from fossil fuel corporations, "a move inspired by Pope Francis' 2015 encyclical."[8] Back in 2016 the encyclical was also praised at a session of faith leaders at the Paris climate negotiations.[9]

The Catholic Social Teaching Tradition

Early in *Laudato si'*, Francis refers to some of his predecessors and their encyclicals. In particular, he notes Popes John XXIII, Paul VI, John Paul II, and Benedict XVI. John XXIII was the first to speak of concerns about water; Paul VI addressed "ecological concerns"; John Paul II called for "global ecological conversion"; and Benedict XVI sought "respect for the environment." Examining the history of CST since 1891 gives a sense of how Francis derived such principles as the common good, the preferential option for the poor, and even the care of creation, among others, which he draws upon in *Laudato si'*.

Pope Leo XIII on Justice for Workers and a Fair Wage

In his 1891 encyclical, *Rerum novarum* (*On the Condition of Labor*), Pope Leo XIII finds the world of his day, namely Europe and the Americas, torn between two evils, unbridled laissez-faire "liberal"

---

7. "News Briefing," *The Tablet*, July 8, 2017, 25.

8. Sarah Tory, "Greening the Gospel," *High Country News*, September 18, 2017, 30.

9. Ibid.

capitalism[10] on the one hand, and a violent form of atheistic socialism on the other. As opposed to the class struggle pictured in socialism, Leo sees the relationship between capitalist and laborer as a cooperation in production. His basic emphasis rests upon the natural rights of workers, rights that arise from the nature of being human and that apply to all,[11] such as a day of rest, shorter working hours, no child labor, and a just wage due as a matter of justice (*RN* 34). Workers also have the natural right to form unions, which must receive the government's protection (*RN* 34, 36). Although this encyclical does not mention water, and the environment is seen as having no other value than to provide benefits for the human community, it does strengthen the need for justice and fairness for all.

Pope Pius XI on Subsidiarity and Social Justice

Pope Pius XI was faced with the painful realities of a worldwide depression, fascist forces in Western Europe, and entrenched communism in the USSR, when he wrote his 1931 encyclical *Quadragesimo anno* (*Reconstruction of the Social Order*). He articulates a vision of society built upon voluntary groups organized by vocation—that is, each company or organization would be comprised of labor and capital, with workers and managers together determining policies for the benefit of all (*QA* 65). Unions, schools, church organizations, and other civil groups provide mediating institutions, negotiating between the isolated individual and the omnipotent state. This arrangement, illuminated in *Quadragesimo anno*, is based on the principle of subsidiarity, which is useful in discussing the water crises.

---

10. Here, *liberal* means freed from the constraints of religion or the state, free to operate with no regulations—in other words a totally free market, no matter the consequences for other elements of society. The term retains the same meaning in Europe today, not its progressive meaning in the United States. *Laissez-faire* refers to a doctrine that promotes economic activity with little government or other interference in order to pursue freedom in economic matters. The two terms are interchangeable.

11. Note that *rights* in the context of CST refers to natural rights or rights of all peoples, rather than civil, political, or economic rights, which are conferred by a state government. For example, in the United States many convicted felons lose their political right to vote. A natural right is a demand or claim by a person or group based in inherent human dignity. Rights are not static but expand according to circumstances of time and place.

Pius XI defines the principle of subsidiarity as "a fundamental principle of social philosophy . . . that one should not withdraw from individuals and commit to the community what they can accomplish by their own enterprise and industry" (*QA* 79).

Finally, economic arrangements must be ruled by the principles of social justice, whereby "one class is forbidden to exclude the other from a share in the profits" so "that the common good of all be thereby promoted" (*QA* 57). This point can be seen in Pope Francis's concern about the domination of rich nations over poor countries.[12]

Effects of the 1891 and 1931 Encyclicals on Workers

The 1891 and 1931 encyclicals by Leo XIII and Pius XI acted as calls for Catholic leaders, activists, and thinkers to embrace the cause of workers in the industrial centers in the United States and Europe. For example, in 1889 in the United Kingdom, Cardinal Manning mediated the London dockworkers strike,[13] while in the United States Fr. John Ryan, theologian and progressive church leader, worked tirelessly to move the US Catholic community in the direction of support for workers. His influence was critical to the 1919 letter of the US bishops, "Program on Social Reconstruction," on the terrible effects of unrestrained capitalism on the poor, workers, and society in general.[14] The bishops challenged unequivocally "insufficient incomes for the great majority of wage earners; and unnecessarily large incomes for a small minority of privileged capitalists."[15]

---

12. See Mich, *Catholic Social Teaching and Movements*, 61–89, for an excellent summary of the document and the times.

13. "News," *The Tablet*, September 23, 2017, 30.

14. For a thorough and important discussion of the influence and importance of Fr. John Ryan, see Mich, *Catholic Social Teaching and Movements*, 55–57. See also the John Ryan Institute for Catholic Social Thought at the University of St. Thomas, St. Paul, MN.

15. Quoted in "This Land Is Home to Me," Pastoral Letter by the Catholic Bishops of Appalachia, 1975, 19, available at *http://ccappal.org/publications/pastoral-letters*. The 1919 document is available at *http://cuomeka.wrlc.org/exhibits/show/bishops/background/1919-bishops-reconstruction*.

Leo XIII's 1891 encyclical and movements by bishops, progressive clergy, and others influenced a number of post-World War I Catholic organizations and people. One of the most famous was Dorothy Day, peace and justice activist and founder of the Catholic Worker movement, which she began to relieve the plight of the poor. She and others published *The Catholic Worker* newspaper and started Houses of Hospitality around the country to take in those least of society, and that work continues to this day.[16]

Pius XI's *Quadragesimo anno* found wide acceptance across Europe as the continent faced the collapse of capitalism in the Great Depression and the rise of a variety of fascist, Nazi, and communist regimes from Spain to the USSR. European Catholic leaders praised the encyclical for its approach to a new social order through intermediary institutions, that is, organizations and groups that provided individuals the opportunity to pursue social justice and economic support by joining toward common goals. Examples include unions, churches, and other groupings that mediated between the individual citizen and an all-encompassing and overarching government as found in fascism or communism.[17]

In 1941, the young priest Jose Maria Arizmendiarrieta arrived in the Mondragon area of northwestern Spain to make a difference in situations of great poverty and hunger. By 1943 inspired by and armed with Pius XI's encyclical, he had established a technical college that trained generations of managers, engineers, and skilled labor using CST as his guideline. The Mondragon Cooperative operated and still operates today on principles of social justice with a particular emphasis upon the sovereignty of labor. Salaries are guided for

---

16. See Dorothy Day's autobiography, *The Long Loneliness;* in 1996 a film was made of her life, *Entertaining Angels*, starring Moira Kelly as Day and Martin Sheen as her coworker Peter Maurin. *The Catholic Worker* newspaper still sells for a penny. For further discussion of Day and other Catholic organizations influenced by the work of Pope Leo and Catholic bishops, see Mich, "Social Catholics in the Unites States" and "The 1930s: Hope Amid Cynicism and Disillusionment," chapters 2 and 3 in *Catholic Social Teaching and Movements* (Mystic, CT: Twenty-Third Publications, 2004).

17. Cf. Eli Witte et al., *Political History of Belgium from 1830 Onwards* (Brussels: Academic and Scientific Publishers, 2009). See especially chapters 2 and 3, "The Triumph of Liberalism (ca. 1850–1884)" and "The Expansion of Democracy (1885–1918)."

all by justice principles. Currently some seventy-five different businesses operate through the Mondragon Cooperative thanks to Fr. Arizmendiarrieta and his implementation of *Quadragesimo anno*.[18] In the United States several Jesuit schools started "labor schools" after World War II to educate workers and labor leaders on the Church's teachings on CST.[19] These are only a few examples of the dramatic influence of these teachings on the Catholic community in the United States and Europe.

Pope John XXIII on the Common Good

There were high expectations in the early 1960s. Former colonies in Africa had gained political independence, and in Europe and Japan, postwar recovery brought new hope for economic development. In Rome, Angelo Giuseppe Roncalli, cardinal and patriarch of Venice, was elected pope in 1958 at age seventy-six. He took the name John XXIII. Expected to be only an interim pope until someone younger could be elected, he surprised all with his dynamic encyclicals and the call for a second Vatican Council.

His first major encyclical, *Mater et magistra* (*Christianity and Social Progress*), issued in 1961, expresses the optimistic theme that the interdependent world is advancing toward a global common good. John XXIII calls upon wealthy countries to aid poorer, nonindustrialized nations. The ultimate goal is the global common good, which he says, "embraces the sum total of those conditions of social living whereby people are enabled more fully and more readily to achieve their own perfection" (*MM* 65).[20] This goal of the common good is a strict demand of social justice, whereby the growth of the economy must parallel a growth in social development of everyone in the community (*MM* 73–74).

---

18. Cf. Roy Morrison, *We Build the Road as We Travel* (Beech River Books, 1991); "Basic Principles of the Mondragon Cooperative Corporation," available on the website of Trade Practices.

19. See information about the Twomey Center for Peace through Justice on the Loyola University New Orleans website, *www.loyno.edu/twomey/about-twomey-center*.

20. This is the only definition of the common good found in CST. Francis extended the common good to include the common good of the environment.

John XXIII sees the need for public authorities to ensure improvements in highway construction, housing, medical services, education, and pure drinking water—the first time water as a specific need is mentioned in CST (*MM* 127); otherwise, John does not address the environment.

Pope John XXIII on Human Rights

In 1963 Pope John XXIII issues another significant document, *Pacem in terris* (*Peace on Earth*). The pope focuses on peace in light of the Korean War, the Berlin Wall, and the Cuban Missile Crisis, which brought the United States and the USSR to the brink of nuclear war. He stresses the need to end the arms race, ban nuclear weapons, and begin disarmament and control of these weapons (*PT* 109–112).

Peace rests upon recognition of the dignity of persons and the rights and duties that emerge from personhood. While a list of rights was developed in 1948 in the United Nations Declaration of Human Rights,[21] John XXIII begins his letter by indicating that fundamental to human dignity are the rights to life, bodily integrity, and "means which are suitable for a proper development of life; these are primarily food, clothing, shelter, rest, and medical care" (*PT* 11). Here water is considered a part of the right to food. These rights are not dependent upon a particular state authority but rest in the dignity of persons.

Second Vatican Council on the Universal Destination of Created Goods

To the surprise of most Catholic leaders and laypeople, John XXIII called upon the bishops of the world to assemble in Rome in 1962

---

21. See *www.un.org/en/universal-declaration-human-rights/* for the full text. Environmental issues went unnoticed in the document; there was no reference to the human right to water. In following decades, several attempts were made to add the right to water to the Declaration, as Article 31, declaring that everyone has the right to "clean and accessible water." The attempts have so far failed, however. See *http://article31.org/*.

for a major reworking of the Catholic Church's response to this new world emerging from the ruins of World War II. This Second Vatican Council (1962–1965)[22] was to "open the windows of the church to the world." The pope's "updating," or *aggiornamento*, is most fully expressed in the council's 1965 document *Gaudium et spes* (*Pastoral Constitution on the Church in the Modern World*).

A new principle emerges in the bishops' deliberations, namely, the universal destination of created goods: "God intended the earth with everything contained in it for the use of all human beings and peoples . . . the right of having a share of earthly goods sufficient for oneself and one's family belongs to everyone" (*GS* 69). There are no direct references to water, although among the fundamental human rights listed are the right to "food, clothing, and shelter" (*GS* 26).

Pope Paul VI on Integral Development, Universal Destination of Created Goods, and the Preferential Option for the Poor

Pope Paul VI began his role as leader of the Church in 1963 and oversaw the completion of the Second Vatican Council. The hopes many people had at the start of the 1960s for the development of poor nations had given way to the hard realization that economic development, far from aiding the poorer nations, actually imposed a new domination by economic interests of wealthy countries.

In Latin America, Paul VI saw the people's poverty and listened to the pleas of a new generation of priests, nuns, and laypeople. Their work, led by Dominican theologian Gustavo Guttierez and others, was rooted in their contact with the poor of Latin America. It was at the 1968 Latin American Episcopal Council (CELAM [Consejo Episcopal Latinoamericano]) conference in Medellin, Colombia, that the leaders of the Church in Latin America pledged to support a "preferential option for the poor."[23] That is, among the

---

22. The First Vatican Council, convened by Pope Pius IX, lasted from 1869 to 1870 and brought bishops from around the world together to react to the rising forces in Europe.

23. See Gustavo Guttierez, *A Theology of Liberation* (Maryknoll, NY: Orbis Books, 1968) for a discussion of this new direction in Catholic theology.

many options the Church has as part of its ministry, there is a preference for working with and for the poor. Hunger and poverty were manifestations of institutionalized violence and could be overcome through public policy. After centuries of seeing their Church allied with the wealthy upper classes supported by the military, the poor saw champions in their priests, bishops, nuns, and laypeople, in pursuit of public policies.

Paul VI takes up these developments in his landmark 1967 encyclical, *Populorum progressio* (*On the Development of Peoples*). The tone is dramatic: inequalities in wealth and power across the globe are a scandal (*PP* 9): "We must make haste; too many are suffering" (*PP* 29); "There are certainly situations whose injustice cries to heaven" (*PP* 30).

Rather than understanding development solely in economic terms, Paul VI espouses a broader approach, namely, integral development, or the promotion of "the good of every man [*sic*] and of the whole man [*sic*]" (*PP* 14, 42).[24] This dynamic understanding, based on the unique dignity of each person and the common good, leads Paul to a sharp criticism of capitalism (*PP* 58).[25]

Paul VI on Political Equality, Participation in Decision Making, and the Option for the Poor

In 1971 Paul VI, in commemorating the eightieth anniversary of *Rerum novarum*, expressed his reflections in *Octogesima adveniens* (*A Call to Action*), an apostolic letter to Cardinal Roy, president of the Pontifical Council for Justice and Peace. The letter is a call for justice through political action in light of "flagrant inequalities . . . in the economic, cultural and political development" of nations (*OA* 2).

---

24. Francis developed this formula into "integral ecology," encompassing the whole Earth.

25. Paul VI's encyclical letter on integral development coincided with the establishment by the US Bishops of the Catholic Campaign for Human Development to support organizations and community efforts for development, not charity, in programs and justice efforts. Cf. Mich, "Challenging Structures," in *Catholic Social Teaching and Movements*, 154–76.

Paul introduces two principles new to the CST tradition: equality of all and participation in decision making. That is, there are fundamental rights to political equality and participation in decisions that impact personal and community life. Paul argues that there is a preferential option for the poor by which the more fortunate are even called upon to renounce their rights "so as to place their goods more generously at the service of others" (*OA* 23).

In a brief section, Paul takes up environmental issues—acknowledging that humans, in their exploitation of nature, risk destroying it through pollution and waste (*OA* 21). The Church must spread the gospel message by taking action for change. Political activity that aims at the common good is one key dimension of Christian engagement in the world.

1971 World Synod of Bishops on the Pursuit of Justice as Integral to the Gospel

In 1971 Pope Paul VI brought together the bishops of the world in a synod, a gathering, held in Rome. In their statement, "Justice in the World," the bishops note the serious injustices that are building "a network of domination, oppression, and abuses" that suppress people from participating in a more just world.

At the end of the introduction, the bishops declare, "Action on behalf of justice and participation in the transformation of the world fully appear to us as a constitutive dimension of the preaching of the Gospel"—there can be no separation between the ministries of the Church and the pursuit of justice. "Or, in other words, of the Church's mission for the redemption of the human race and its liberation from every oppressive situation" (introduction, para. 7). The use of the words "liberation from every oppressive situation" is a specific tool to evaluate the Church in the modern world: that is, beyond charity to justice engagement.

The bishops also note the environment—that the natural goods of Earth, "the precious treasures of air and water," "the small delicate biosphere of the whole complex of life on earth, are not infinite" (chap. 1, para. 2). Richer nations have no right "to keep up their claim to increase their own material needs, if the consequence is either that others remain in misery or that the danger of destroying the very physical foundations of life on earth itself is precipitated" ("International Action," 7).

Pope John Paul II on Concern, Respect for All Beings, Social Sin, and Solidarity

In 1978, the cardinal electors chose Karol Wojtyla of Poland as pope. He took the name John Paul II and served until his death in 2005. He was the first non-Italian chosen since the sixteenth century.

In his 1987 encyclical *Sollicitudo rei socialis* (*On Social Concern*), John Paul expresses awareness of the dangers to the environment from industrial development. Development has a "moral character" that includes an "ecological concern," (*SRS* 26) which has three dimensions. First, it includes a growing awareness that humans cannot use beings, "whether living or inanimate—animals, plants, the natural elements—simply as one wishes," according to economic need. Second, the natural world and natural goods are limited; some are even not renewable. And third, development involves issues surrounding the quality of life (*SRS* 34). Respect for all beings, limited natural goods, pollution, and human health—these are key aspects of an ecological outlook and key to a discussion of issues surrounding water.

According to John Paul II, the path forward involves solidarity in relationships among all nations. Solidarity is "a firm and persevering determination to commit oneself to the common good; that is to say to the good of all and of each individual because we are all really responsible for all" (*SRS* 38, 39).

He notes that a culture of consumption with no regard for the environment has developed. He then reiterates the principles of the preferential option for the poor and integral development, first employed by Paul VI. Finally, he argues that as an "expert in humanity" (*SRS* 41), the Church is not just able to comment on human welfare issues but is morally obligated to defend human dignity and the common good.

John Paul II on Earth as Common Heritage and the Human Obligation to Care for Earth

In his January 1, 1990, World Day of Peace address *The Ecological Crisis: A Common Responsibility*, John Paul II turns his full attention to the environmental crisis.[26] He begins by arguing that world peace itself is threatened "by a lack of *due respect for nature*, by the plundering of natural resources" (*WDP* 1) The key to the address is the declaration that the ecological crisis is a moral problem, more than a technological, economic, or political one. The pope connects harm to the environment and harm to humans, particularly in addressing the structural dimensions of poverty. This is a central link addressed by successive popes and bishops. Both ecological harm and the scandal of poverty have become parts of the economic, political, and social structures of the globe. The recourse is "*the urgent moral need for a new solidarity*," a new arrangement among states (*WDP* 6).

John Paul II speaks of Earth as a common heritage "endowed with its own integrity, its own internal, dynamic balance" (*WDP* 7, 8). Earth is not only an instrument for human use and betterment but also it has intrinsic value of its own. The pope concludes with a reminder to Catholics, in particular, "of their serious obligation to care for all of creation" (*WDP* 14–16). Addressing ecological crises by one's actions is no longer merely a *choice*, it is a firm *obligation*.

The applications of John Paul II's address can be seen in the following story. The Sisters of Charity of San Antonio, Texas, owned the headwaters of the much polluted San Antonio River; and as owners of the University of the Incarnate Word, in San Antonio, the Sisters had allowed large parts of the spring's watershed to be turned into athletic fields. But finally in 2002 moved by John Paul II's "Ecological Crisis" statement of 1990, the Sisters saw

---

26. John Paul II, *The Ecological Crisis: A Common Responsibility: Message of His Holiness Pope John Paul II for the Celebration of the World Day of Peace, 1 January 1990* (Vatican City: United States Catholic Conference, 1990), *https://w2.vatican.va/content /john-paul-ii/en/messages/peace/documents/hf_jp-ii_mes_19891208_xxiii-world-day -for-peace.html.*

their work as caring not just for people but also for the river; this was a religious calling.[27]

Then in 2001, US and Canadian bishops of the Columbia Watershed Region in western Washington State and British Columbia proclaimed that Catholics had a responsibility to God to protect the Columbia and its tributaries. The bishops of both countries had worked for five years in conversation with a wide variety of stakeholders from farmers to environmentalists. Their final document[28] was strengthened by the writings of John Paul II.

John Paul II on Natural and Social Ecology

In 1991, one hundred years after the publication of *Rerum novarum*, John Paul II issued his social encyclical, *Centesimus annus* (*On the Hundredth Anniversary of Rerum novarum*). Although he celebrates the 1987 collapse of communism in the former USSR and its European satellites, the pope critiques the rise of a consumer society in the West (*CA* 32–33). The capitalist free market system has emerged as the most efficient instrument for using nature's goods; yet many needs, such as food and water, find no place in the market. Justice demands that those needs do not go unsatisfied. Consequently, the market must be appropriately controlled (*CA* 35).

Finally, the document looks at the environment in terms of the trends of consumerist societies, which create artificial needs for the purpose of selling nonnecessities, "often damaging to . . . physical and spiritual health" (*CA* 36). The result is that people consume the goods of Earth, such as water, in "an excessive and disordered way" (*CA* 37). The environment has its own requisites and purposes, before human uses. Along with the destruction of the natural environment, the pope singles out the "serious destruction of the *human environment*" (*CA* 37–39). Natural ecology and social ecology are linked.

---

27. Cynthia Barnett, *Blue Revolution: Unmaking America's Water Crisis* (Boston: Beacon Press, 2011), 213.

28. "The Columbia River Watershed: Caring for Creation and the Common Good," *www.thewscc.org/uploads/3/4/9/4/34945816/colrvr-e.pdf.*

New Forms of Environmental Concern in CST

Human Rights—Pontifical Council for Justice and Peace, 2003–2006

The Vatican's Pontifical Council for Justice and Peace addressed the Third World Water Forum in Kyoto, Japan, in March 2003. The forum is a gathering of world leaders advocating the merits of privatizing water. The PCJP's statement paid particular attention to the link between water and poverty: "Many people living in poverty . . . daily face enormous hardship because water supplies are neither sufficient nor safe. Women bear a disproportionate hardship."

The problem is viewed not as one of scarcity but of "distribution and resources." There is clearly a link between ethical principles and water: "Access and deprivation underlie most water decisions. Hence linkages between water policy and ethics increasingly emerge throughout the world."[29]

In 2004, the PCJP followed up, arguing that water is not just another commodity with only economic value. Even if entrusted to private enterprises, water remains a public good, so necessary is it to life: "The right to water, as all human rights, finds its basis in human dignity. Without water, life is threatened. Therefore water is a human right."[30] The Council repeated the same concerns at the Fourth World Water Forum in Mexico City, in March 2006.[31]

Benedict XVI on Integral Development, Preferential Option for the Poor, and Universal Destination of Goods

After John Paul II's death in April 2005, Joseph Cardinal Ratzinger was elected pope and took the name Benedict XVI. He served until his resignation in 2013, one of the few popes to resign from office.

---

29. "Global Water Crisis: A Test of Solidarity," *National Catholic Reporter*, May 30, 2003, 32.

30. Laura Vargas, "A Common Good," *Scarboro Missions Magazine*, September 2004, *www.scarboromissions.ca.*

31. "In Brief," *The Tablet*, March 25, 2006, 41.

His only social encyclical was *Caritas in veritate* (*Charity in Truth*), which was issued in 2009.

Intended as a reflection on Paul VI's *Populorum progressio* of 1967, Benedict examines the key principles of integral development, preferential option for the poor, and the universal destination of the goods of Earth in light of ongoing globalization, increasing marginalization, large-scale migration, and continued exploitation of Earth's natural goods for the benefit of a few.

Here Benedict reminds us that people are responsible for the natural environment, the poor, and future generations. If we do not respect the intrinsic balance of creation, we will abuse the natural world. Far from being solely at the service of human economic interests, the environment exists before human habitation and provides the setting for our life. "Thus it [the environment] too is a 'vocation'" (*CV* 48).[32] Nature is at our disposal as a "gift of the Creator who has given it an inbuilt order, enabling man [*sic*] to draw from it the principles needed in order 'to till it and keep it' (Gen 2:15)" (*CV* 48).

All projects to promote development "need to be *marked by solidarity and inter-generational justice*, while taking into account a variety of contexts: ecological, juridical, economic, political and cultural." In this process, the preferential option for the poor must be paramount (*CV* 48–49). When wealthier nations stockpile natural goods, which are often found in poorer countries, the result is greater exploitation of people and the environment.

Benedict invites societies to examine lifestyles in relation to the disease of consumerism. In this regard, the Catholic Church has "a responsibility towards creation. . . . In so doing, she must defend not only earth, water, and air as gifts of creation that belong to everyone. She must above all protect mankind [*sic*] from self-destruction." Benedict thus links human ecology and natural ecology. Harm to nature means harm to culture, and the contrary is also true (*CV* 51).

Integral development, the integrity of creation, human ecology, consumerism, protection of Earth, water, and air are now linked in a strong moral argument in Benedict's writings and in the Church's interventions at the World Water Forums. As shown earlier, Francis works these elements into a powerful and coherent whole.

---

32. *CV* 48 references John Paul II, *Message for the 1990 World Day of Peace*, 6.

Summary

CST Documents Referenced in This Chapter[33]

Year	Author	Title	Major Theme
1891	Leo XIII	Rerum novarum (On the Condition of Labor)	Labor justice
1931	Pius XI	Quadragesimo anno (Reconstruction of the Social Order)	Social justice, subsidiarity
1961	John XXIII	Mater et magistra (Christianity and Social Progress)	Common good
1963	John XXIII	Pacem in terris (Peace on Earth)	Dignity, rights
1965	Vatican II	Gaudium et spes (Pastoral Constitution on the Church in the Modern World)	Universal destination of goods
1967	Paul VI	Populorum progressio (On the Development of Peoples)	Integral development
1971	Paul VI	Octogesima adveniens (Call to Action)	Participation, option for poor
1971	Synod of Bishops	Justice in the World	Gospel justice, precious water
1987	John Paul II	Sollicitudo rei socialis (On Social Concern)	Solidarity
1990	John Paul II	World Day of Peace	Care for Creation
1991	John Paul II	Centesimus annus (On the Hundredth Anniversary of Rerum novarum)	Natural and social ecology linked
2009	Benedict XVI	Caritas in veritate (Charity in Truth)	Protecting the environment
2015	Francis	Laudato si': On Care for Our Common Home	Earth: our common home

33. Quotes from the encyclicals by Popes Leo XIII, Pius XI, John XXIII, and Paul VI (*Rerum Novarum, Quadragesimo anno, Mater et magistra, Pacem in terris, Populorum progressio, Octogesima adveniens*) are from David J. O'Brien and Thomas A. Shannon, *Catholic Social Thought: The Documentary Heritage* (Maryknoll, NY: Orbis Books, 1992). Quotes from *Gaudium et spes, Justice in the World,* Pope John Paul II's *1990 World Day of Peace* message, and the encyclicals by Popes John Paul II, Benedict XVI, and Francis (*Sollicitudo rei socialis, Centesimus annus, Caritas in veritate, Laudato si'*) are from *www.vatican.va*.

CST is committed to justice—justice for workers, for the poor, and for Earth. Although much more can be said, it is important to realize that the movement has developed from regarding the environment and water as mere instruments of human benefit and improvement to regarding them as central to CST. Water and the environment have an integrity and purpose of their own. Water is not just included in the right to food, as articulated by John XXIII but is a right in itself, as outlined by the Pontifical Council for Justice and Peace and Pope Francis.

The principles in the CST documents of the early twenty-first century that come into play in responding to water crises are as follow:

- Universal destination of created goods, with a focus on the poor and marginalized
- Preferential option for the poor, especially in light of the super-abundance of wealthy nations, and wealthy people, and the degradation of the environment
- Integral ecology, expanded from the term *integral development*, which is the intersection of the natural environment and the human environment
- Common good, now including the good of the entire Earth and all its creatures—inorganic and organic matter
- Need for a new spirituality, conversion, and ecological education brought about by an acute awareness of the ecological harm to Earth and thus to human communities
- Cultural integrity, in particular the cultures of indigenous peoples threatened by unregulated economic intrusions into their territories and ancient practices

These are the principles that chapters 2–8 use to examine climate change, pollution, extractive enterprises, privatization, the misuse of Earth's goods, the right to water, and water's rights, all in relation to the global water crises.[34]

---

34. This discussion has not included critical evaluation of CST. For those discussions, see John Coleman, ed., *One Hundred Years of Catholic Social Thought* (Maryknoll, NY: Orbis Books, 1991), and Donal Dorr, *Option for the Poor and for the Earth* (Maryknoll, NY: Orbis Books, 2012); Paul Sullins and Anthony Blasi, eds, *Catholic Social Thought: American Reflections on the Compendium* (Lanham, MD: Rowman and Littlefield, 2009); and Kenneth Himes, ed., *Modern Catholic Social Teaching: Commentaries and Interpretations* (Washington, DC: Georgetown Press, 2004).

Review Questions

1. Why were the popes opposed to socialism in the early encyclicals?
2. What rights do workers have in CST writings? What are the basic rights of all people? And what is the grounding for those rights?
3. What principles does Paul VI add to CST?
4. What are the objections of the popes to capitalism?
5. What is the source of the principle of the preferential option for the poor? How is the principle used in later documents?
6. What is the meaning of the *common good*?
7. What is the meaning of *solidarity*?

Discussion Questions

1. How would you introduce Catholic social teaching to people unfamiliar with it?
2. Which document introduced in this chapter most interests you? Explain why and what about it has challenged or moved you.
3. In what ways, if any, have Catholic social teachings informed your view of the world or challenged you?
4. Do the writings provide a "middle ground" between unrestrained capitalism and communism or socialism? Explain.

CHAPTER

Climate Change as Structural Violence[1]

Just five miles off the coast of Alaska's Seward Peninsula lies the small island of Sarichef, inhabited by about six hundred Inupiat indigenous people. The island's only village, Shishmaref, has been their home for centuries. Inhabitants subsist by hunting, which has meant driving on dogsleds and snowmobiles across sea ice.

In the early 1980s, hunters noticed the sea ice changing: forming later in the fall and breaking up earlier in spring. Driving on the ice became dangerous. The village became more vulnerable to storms. After strong storms hit in 2001 and 2002, the villagers reluctantly

---

1. I owe the concept of climate change as "structural violence" to Kevin O'Brien, Catholic ethicist at Pacific Lutheran University, Tacoma, Washington, who delivered a presentation, "Christian Nonviolence as a Response to Climate Change," at the Just Sustainability conference, "Hope for the Commons," Seattle University, August 4–6, 2016.

The term *structural violence* here relates to the impacts of climate change not only to Earth but also especially to poor and vulnerable communities. The "violence" is visited upon them by the consumption patterns of the wealthy members of Earth communities who have water in abundance, greater access to consumer goods, and an overall access to good health. *Structural* does not refer to individuals as individuals but rather to the ways in which people and their societies structure their consumptive habits. Chapter 2 will examine some of these points and emphasize Pope Francis's encyclical *Laudato si': On Care for Our Common Home* as an ethical call to change patterns of production and consumption in relation to climate change. This chapter moves from a description of climate change and its impacts, especially in relation to water in the skies and on Earth, to the ethical framework provided in CST.

Scientist and environmental activist Vandana Shiva uses the term *climate chaos* because *climate change* "suggests predictability, and change in itself is not a bad thing." *Water Wars: Privatization, Pollution, and Profit* (Berkeley, CA: North Atlantic Books, 2016), xvi.

The island of Kiribati is hit often by flooding from rising sea levels.

voted to move the entire village to the mainland—to a remote site without roads or nearby towns—before the sea could claim the island completely.[2]

The complications of global warming are also evident in the Central Pacific island of Kiribati. Signs involve flooding, erosion, unpredictable rainfall, and increasingly salty groundwater. The National Aeronautics and Space Administration (NASA) reported that from 1992 to 2014 sea levels there rose three inches on average per year during that period.[3] The United Nations Intergovernmental Panel on Climate Change (IPCC) predicts that sea-level rises are inevitable and that within a century Kiribati's useful land will be largely submerged, making it impossible for people to stay on the island.

Kiribati's president Tong recently visited wealthier countries, asking them to cut their carbon emissions. He also persuaded his

2. Elizabeth Kolbert, "Disappearing Islands, Thawing Permafrost, Melting Polar Ice: How the Earth Is Changing," *New Yorker*, April 25, 2005, *www.newyorker.com /magazine/2005/04/25/the-climate-of-man-islands*. Three other Alaskan coastal villages are also in danger due to erosion and storm surges caused by melting sea ice. See Elizabeth Shogren, "Interior's Lonely Whistleblower," *High Country News*, November 27, 2017, 28.

3. NASA, "Scientific Consensus: Earth's Climate Is Warming," *Global Climate Change: Vital Signs of the Planet, https://climate.nasa.gov/climate_resources/145/.*

nation's parliament to put aside $8.7 million to buy 5,500 acres in Fiji. Most islanders have joined the effort to organize for the move, and many were inspired by Pope Francis's call for climate change action.[4]

What Is Climate Change?

The scientific consensus is that the climate of our planet is changing, and that human activity is playing a significant role in this change. This chapter concerns the impact of climate change and global warming on Earth's waters. According to NASA, *global warming* "refers to the long-term warming of the planet," a well-documented rise "since the early twentieth century." *Climate change* is a broad term that "encompasses global warming, but refers to the broader range of changes that are happening to our planet," such as "rising sea levels, shrinking mountain glaciers, accelerating ice melt." These result from "warming, which is caused mainly by people burning fossil fuels and putting out heat-trapping gases into the air." The following is a short list of gases that contribute to the greenhouse effect, that is, warming "that results when the atmosphere traps heat radiating from Earth," like a blanket around Earth:

- water vapor
- carbon dioxide (CO_2)
- methane (largely from decomposition of wastes in landfills, agriculture, ruminant digestion, and manure management of animals)
- nitrous oxide (from use of fertilizers, fossil fuel combustion, biomass burning)
- chlorofluorocarbons (CFCs) (synthetic compounds used in industrial production)[5]

---

4. Mike Ives, "A Matter of Faith," *Sierra Magazine* 101.6 (November/December, 2016): 41–43, 50. See also Aaron Packard, *Huffington Post, March 12, 2015, www. huffingtonpost.com/aaron-packard/the-unfolding-crisis-in-kiribati-and-the-urgency -of-response_b_6854386.html.*

5. NASA, "Frequently Asked Questions," "Causes: A blanket around the Earth," *https://climate/nasa.gov.*

The top image shows Muir Glacier, Glacier Bay National Park and Preserve, Alaska, in 1941. The bottom image captures the same area in 2004. From 1941 to 2004 the glacier retreated thirty-one miles. Note the lack of floating ice and presence of abundant vegetation.

The National Oceanic and Atmospheric Administration (NOAA), reported that 2016 was the hottest year ever recorded with the highest greenhouse gas marks and record sea levels.[6] An October

6. Steve Almasy, CNN News, August 10, 2017, *www.cnn.com/2017/08/10/us/noaa-2016-climate-change-report/index.html*; Justin Gillis, "Earth Sets a Temperature Record for the Third Straight Year," *www.nytimes.com/2017/01/18/science/earth-highest-temperature-record.html?_r=0*.

2017 report from the World Meteorological Organization (WMO) stated that 2016 showed "record global temperatures, exceptionally low sea ice, and unabated sea-level rise and ocean heat. Extreme weather and climate conditions have continued into 2017."[7]

The 2014 report of the IPCC concluded, "Human influence on the climate system is clear, and recent anthropogenic [human caused] emissions of greenhouse gases are the highest in history."[8] This conclusion is strongly supported by more than 97 percent of the scientific community.

NASA has reached the same conclusion: "Observations throughout the world make it clear that climate change is occurring, and rigorous scientific research demonstrates that the greenhouse gases emitted by human activities are the primary driver."[9]

Effects of Climate Change

The "violence" of climate change involves the differing impacts of climate change in different parts of the world and within the United States. As a recent study in the journal *Science* points out, "climate change tends to increase pre-existing inequality." Some of the poorest parts of the globe, as well as the poorest regions of the southwest and southeast United States, could see "the largest economic losses." Those regions already hot will experience even greater warming.[10]

National security experts are concerned about impacts of climate change on resources and countries, especially in the drier regions of the world, such as sub-Saharan Africa. President Trump's Secretary of Defense, James Mattis, testified in March 2017 to the Senate

---

7. "Statement on the Status of the Global Climate in 2016," World Meteorological Organization, October 30, 2017, *https://public.wmo.int/en/media/press-release /climate-breaks-multiple-records-2016-global-impacts.*

8. IPCC, "Fifth Assessment Report (AR5), Summary for Policymakers (2014)," *ipcc.ch/pdf/assessment-report/ar5/syr/AR5_SYR_FINAL_SPM.pdf.*

9. NASA, *Global Climate Change: Vital Signs of the Planet, http://climate.nasa.gov /scientific-consensus.*

10. Brad Plumer and Nadja Popovich, "As Climate Changes, Southern States Will Suffer More Than Others," *New York Times,* June 29, 2017, *www.nytimes.com/interactive /2017/06/29/climate/southern-states-worse-climate effects.html.*

Armed Services Committee, that "climate change is impacting stability in areas of the world where our troops are operating today. It is appropriate to incorporate drivers of instability that impact the security environment into planning."[11]

How Climate Change Works

As mentioned previously, various human activities ranging from industrial emissions to exhaust fumes from cars and poor farming and ranching practices release carbon dioxide, methane, and nitrous oxide into the atmosphere, where they linger. Although most gases settle into oceans, the rest are emitted into the air. The more greenhouse gases (GHGs) emitted, the more solar heat is trapped in Earth's atmosphere, forming a hot blanket around the planet. The more heat that can't escape, the hotter things get for life on Earth.

NASA reported that on September 10, 2016, Arctic sea ice hit its lowest annual extent. The average extent of Arctic sea ice has dropped steadily every month since 1978.[12] The role the Arctic sea ice plays in climate change is critical. The ice reflects back 80 percent of the sunlight that hits it, but when the ice melts, the darker ocean absorbs about 90 percent of this sunlight. Warming oceans mean more ice melts. The feedback loop continues—melt, absorb, warm, melt, absorb, warm. In 2014, researchers reported that the Arctic would be ice-free by 2050.[13]

---

11. Andrew Revkin, "Trump's Defense Secretary Cites Climate Change as National Security Challenge," *ProPublica*, March 14, 2017, *www.propublica.org/article /trumps-defense-secretary-cites-climate-change-national-security-challenge*.

12. "Seven Climate Change Records Broken," Climate Reality Project, October 12, 2016, *www.climaterealityproject.org/blog/seven-climate-change-records-broken -2016?utm_source Email*.

13. Alex Kozoian, producer, "Animated Map Shows What the United States Would Look Like If All Ice Melted," *Business Insider*, November 30, 2015, *www .businessinsider.com/united-states-looks-like-earths-ice-melted-climate-change-gl*. See also Allen Best, "Glaciers Offer a Glimpse of the Distant Past," in *High and Dry: Dispatches on Global Warming from the American West* (Boulder, CO: *High Country News*, 2006). Best notes that ice cores from Greenland ice sheets show that carbon dioxide (CO_2) and other greenhouse gases have risen by 30 percent in the past 250 years, 7–8, 16.

Impact: Sea Level Rises and Severe Weather

In Alaska, six indigenous villages will most likely be submerged as sea levels rise and storms intensify. One estimate indicates that millions of the nearly one billion people worldwide, mostly the poor who live in low-lying river deltas, will have to migrate as the seas submerge their homelands.[14]

In June 2016, Norfolk, Virginia, experienced such flooding that vertical rulers were installed so people could judge whether they could drive on roads hit by tidal floods. In that same year, five hundred miles south, the only road to Tybee Island, Georgia, disappeared at times under the rising sea.[15] Indeed, large-scale flooding seems inevitable, and freshwater sources are threatened as rising seas leave coastal groundwater areas salty. For the most part those threatened tend to be the poor and the vulnerable who live in areas prone to storm surges and flooding.

As seas have warmed, the weather has become more severe. Hurricanes and typhoons are stronger, absorbing more energy from warmer waters. Rainfall is heavier; storm surges are stronger. Those living inland are not spared from the impacts of climate change. With a warmer atmosphere, clouds hold more water vapor and drop more rain, thus increasing flooding.[16]

The year 2017 saw some of the fiercest hurricanes in recent years. First hurricane Harvey plowed into Houston, Texas, in late August, as a category 4 hurricane, bringing not just coastal flooding but also intense rain for days. By one estimate the storm dropped 24.5 trillion gallons of water on Texas and Louisiana. Next, in September 2017 the destruction brought by intense hurricanes unfolded dramatically when hurricane Irma, a category 5, hit the Caribbean before rolling into Florida with coastal surge flooding and flooding rainfalls. Then came the devastating hurricane Maria, another category 5 hurricane,

---

14. Ibid.

15. Justin Gills, "Flooding of Coast by Global Warming Has Already Begun," *New York Times*, September 3, 2016, *www.nytimes.com/2016/09/04/science/flooding-of-coast -caused-by-global-warming-has-already-begun.html?*

16. See "A Handy Refresher on the Basics of Climate Change," Climate Reality Project, October 24, 2016, *www.climaterealityproject.org/blog/handy-refresher-basics -climate-change.*

which destroyed much of Puerto Rico and the Virgin Islands, forcing many citizens to flee to the mainland.[17] Though scientists cannot say that climate change causes hurricanes, they can say that climate change makes hurricanes more destructive.

Then in the same month of September, California was hit by more than seventeen fire outbreaks, resulting in wide destruction, particularly in the Santa Rosa area north of San Francisco. Were the fires related to climate change? Although a definitive answer has yet to emerge, there is indeed evidence of such a connection. Scott Stephens, professor of fire science at the University of California, Berkeley, sees climate change as "a key part of the [fire] equation."[18] Climate change has multiple sources and impacts.[19]

Climate Change

Even if humanity stopped emitting greenhouse gases today, climate change would continue for a considerable time, with anthropogenic, that is, human caused, pollution staying in the atmosphere for hundreds of years. However, if humanity does nothing, the global average temperature could rise by 6 degrees Celsius (10.8 degrees Fahrenheit) by the end of the century. If the global average surface temperature were to rise this high over preindustrial levels, "most of the planetary surface would be functionally uninhabitable," according to author, journalist, and environmental activist Mark Lynas, who focuses on climate change.[20]

---

17. Brian Donegan and Jonathan Erdman, "September 2017 Was the Most Active Month on Record for Atlantic Hurricanes," The Weather Channel, September 30, 2017, *https://weather.com/storms/hurricane/news/september-2017-most-active-month-on-record-for-atlantic-hurricanes*; "Up to Speed," *Sierra*, November/December 2017, 20.

18. Katy Steinmetz, "The Fire Season," *Time*, October 23, 2017, 42.

19. The Times Editorial Board, "The Climate-change Fire Alarm from Northern California," *Los Angeles Times*, October 12, 2017, *www.latimes.com/opinion/editorials/la-ed-northern-california-fires-20171012-story.html*.

20. Mark Lynas is the author of *Six Degrees: Our Future on a Hotter Planet* (Washington, DC: *National Geographic*, 2007). The quotation is from "A Handy Refresher on the Basics of Climate Change," Climate Reality Project, October 24, 2016, *www.climaterealityproject.org/blog/handy-refresher-basics-climate-change*.

Impact: Acidic Waters

The rising level of carbon dioxide (CO_2) in the atmosphere is making the oceans more acidic. CO_2 in the ocean forms carbonic acid and prevents the development of carbonate, which is key to the formation of calcium carbonate shells for shellfish, marine snails, and coral reefs. The dramatic rise in global CO_2 emissions in recent decades has raised the ocean's acidity to levels that are harming or killing marine life. The higher the level of atmospheric CO_2, the higher the acidity of oceans.[21]

Impact: Harm to Coral Reefs

As Earth's waters warm and become more acidic, the health of reefs filled with colorful, sculptural coral weakens or fails. In a November 2016 study, scientists found that more than two-thirds of the coral in Australia's Great Barrier Reef's northern region had died in the previous nine months. It is possible that, by 2050, increasing acidification and warmer ocean temperatures will result in the death or destruction of coral reefs worldwide, which are crucial to the existence of countless other marine species.[22]

Impact: Rain, Snow, and More

Future changes in rainfall patterns, runoff amounts, and soil moisture pose serious challenges to managing water resources. In addition, climate change means less snow in many mountain ranges. Less snow for a shorter period of the year will result in seasonal streams filling up earlier and drying out sooner, higher risk of wildfires, less time for pollination and animal hibernation, weakened ecosystems, and increased opportunistic invasion by nonnative species.[23]

---

21. Sandi Doughton, "Acidified Seawater Too Close, Too Soon," *Seattle Times*, May 23, 2008, A1, 13.

22. Quoted in Juliet Eliperin, "Growing Acidity of Oceans May Kill Corals," *Washington Post*, July 5, 2006, A1; "Milestones," *Time*, December 12, 2016, 19. See also Justin Worland, "The Great Barrier Reef Is under Attack from El Nino and Climate Change," *Time*, April 13, 2016, 14–16.

23. Michelle Nijhuis, "What Happened to Winter?" in *High and Dry: Dispatches on Global Warming from the American West* (Lander, WY: High Country News, 2006), 25–26, 28–29; Sharon Begley, "Global Warming Is a Cause of This Year's Extreme Weather," *Newsweek*, July 14, 2008, 53.

The Himalayan glaciers are also shrinking, with a possible loss of four-fifths of their mass by 2030. The eastern and central glaciers, home to nine of the ten world's highest peaks, are experiencing rapid meltdowns.[24] This would effectively eliminate natural reservoir-storing water for more than a billion people in these areas of the world.

The US national parks are already experiencing climate change three times faster than the rest of the country. In Yosemite, pine trees are growing in formerly subalpine meadows. These thirsty trees dry up the wet meadows, which frustrates small creatures like marmots, frogs, and salamanders looking for food and water. Climate change is "melting glaciers, hastening snowmelt, intensifying wildfires, and pushing animals and plants out of their usual locations. In coming decades, climate change will magnify these impacts."[25]

Impact: Carbon Emissions Increase

In a vicious circle, as climate change melts more ice, exposing previously ice-covered soil, and thaws permafrost, particularly above the Arctic Circle and Greenland, massive amounts of methane and other greenhouse gases (GHGs) will be released into the atmosphere—causing seventeen times more GHG emissions by 2050 than scientists had predicted. This contributes to increased greenhouse gas effects and warming. The loop intensifies.[26]

In effect the whole hydrologic cycle intensifies. The results are heavier rainfalls, more flash flooding, a northward drift of

---

24. Kamran Shaw, "Shrinking 'Himalayan' Glaciers Ignite Fresh 'Climate Change' Concerns—Report," *Inquisitr*, News, November 30, 2015, *www.inquisitr.com/2598783/shrinking-himalayan-glaciers-ignite-fresh-climate-change-concerns-report/*. Also see Vandana Shiva, *Water Wars: Privatization, Pollution, and Profit* (Berkeley, CA: North Atlantic Books, 2016), xvii-xxi, for a discussion of the water crises related to the Himalayan river system.

25. Elizabeth Shogren, "Vital Signs: What Climate Change Is Doing to the Parks," *High Country News*, August 22, 2016, 10, 11–13.

26. T. Crowther et al., "Quantifying Global Soil Carbon Losses in Response to Global Warming," *Science*, December 2016, as quoted in Lindsay Dodgson, "A Bunch of Carbon Dioxide That's Been Trapped in the Soil Is Starting to Escape, and It's Bad News for the Planet," *Business Insider*, October 27, 2016, *www.businessinsider.com/science*.

semitropical plants and animals, "radical reductions in the number of zooplankton near the ocean surface," and "sharp declines in mid-ocean nutrient levels," creating food shortages for deep-ocean creatures.[27]

Climate Refugees

In southern Florida, the residents of Isle de Jean Charles already face dramatic changes to their livelihoods and culture. Once the island environment offered a rich resource for fishing, hunting, and farming to its indigenous inhabitants. Today, more than 90 percent of the island has been washed away.

In January 2016, the people of Isle de Jean Charles received a $48 million grant from the Department of Housing and Urban Development (HUD) to move the last sixty residents from the island. This marked the first use of US federal tax dollars to move a whole people hit by climate change.

The United Nations University Institute for Environment and Human Security and the International Organization for Migration estimate that by 2050 fifty to 200 million people—mostly subsistence farmers and fishermen, the world's most vulnerable and poorest victims of the structural violence of climate change—could be forced to abandon their homes.[28]

Deniers Are Around

Influential deniers and skeptics of human–caused climate change include individuals with powerful public voices. Former Oklahoma Senator Scott Pruitt, now in charge of the Environmental Protection Agency (EPA) under President Donald Trump, has often expressed

---

27. De Villiers, *Water*, 79–80.

28. Coral Davenport and Campbell Robertson, "Resettling the First Climate Refugees," *New York Times*, May 3, 2016, A1, *www.nytimes.com/2016/05/03/us/resettling -the-first-american-climate-refugees.html*. See also Rob Nixon, *Slow Violence and the Environmentalism of the Poor* (Cambridge: Harvard University Press, 2011).

his skepticism that carbon dioxide is a major factor in global warming. The president has tweeted or noted several times that he does not believe in human-caused climate change. In 2015, for example, he stated: "I'm not a believer in man-made global warming. But the problem we have, and if you look at our energy costs, and all of the things that we're doing to solve a problem that I don't think in any major fashion exists."[29]

Jim Inhofe, Republican senator from Oklahoma, opined that humans cannot control the climate, only God can, "The arrogance of people to think that we, human beings, would be able to change what He is doing in the climate is to me outrageous."[30] Another denier joined Inhofe: House representative from Michigan Tim Wahlberg argued that if climate change were "real" God would "take care of" it.[31] Scott Wagner, Republican state senator in Pennsylvania, stated that climate change is caused by humans' "warm bodies."[32]

In March 2016, the Center for American Progress Action Fund noted that in 2015 thirty-nine Republican senators and 144 representatives denied or challenged the science behind human-caused climate change.[33]

Then there are the voices of oil and gas industry representatives. Exxon Mobil is facing charges by the Rockefeller Foundation that Exxon Mobil knew, at least as far back as 1979, that human activity caused climate change.[34] The charge, which Exxon

29. Chris Cillizza, CNN Editor-at-large, "Donald Trump Doesn't Think Much of Climate Change, in 20 Quotes," August 8, 2017, *www.cnn.com/2017/08/08/politics /trump-global-warming/index.html.*

30. Quoted in Cynthia Barnett, *Rain: A Natural and Cultural History* (New York: Broadway Books, 2016), 275.

31. "No, God Won't Take Care of Climate Change," *High Country News,* August 21, 2017, 3.

32. "Up to Speed," *Sierra Magazine,* July/August 2017, 22

33. "Here Are the 56 Percent of Congressional Republicans Who Deny Climate Change," Moyers and Company, February 3, 2015, *http://billmoyers.com/2015/02/03 /congress-climate-deniers/.*

34. See David Kaiser and Lee Wasserman, "The Rockefeller Family Fund vs. Exxon," *New York Review,* December 8, 2016, *www.nybooks.com/articles/2016/12/08 /the-rockefeller-family-fund-vs-exxon/.*

Mobil denies, states that the corporation's directors and scientists knew that burning fossil fuels alters the climate and threatens the future of life on Earth, and that they buried this knowledge and actively campaigned to sow doubt about the reality of climate change among the public.[35] New York and Massachusetts state attorneys general are investigating charges that the company "knowingly deceived the public and shareholders about climate change."[36]

Pope Francis calls such climate change deniers "stupid." Returning via plane from a visit to Colombia, South America, the pope responded to a question of why governments act quickly on matters about arms and weapons but not on the environment. Francis replied: "There's a phrase in the Old Testament . . . where it says that man [sic] is stupid; he's stubborn and does not see." Those who doubt climate change should consult scientists. "They are the most clear. Theirs is not an airy-fairy opinion. Then let the person decide, and history will judge."[37]

In spite of many pleas and objections from business leaders, politicians even in the president's own party, and some Cabinet members, President Donald Trump announced that the United States was withdrawing from the historic 2015 Paris Agreement.[38]

---

35. "Holding Exxon Accountable for Decades of Deception," *Corporate Accountability International* 2 (2016): 1.

36. Quoted in John S. Szalasny, "Another Voice: ExxonMobil Has a History of Denying Climate Change," *Buffalo News*, December 5, 2016, Opinion, *http://buffalo news.com/2016/12/05/another-voice-exxonmobil-history-denying-climate-change/*; see also Ans Kolk, David Levy, "Winds of Change: Corporate Strategy, Climate Change and Oil Multinationals," *European Management Journal* 19 (October 2001), *www. sciencedirect.com/science/article/pii/S0263237301000640*. Recently, under the leadership of now former Secretary of State Rex Tillerson, Exxon to its credit publicly supported the Paris agreement on climate change and reversed its climate denial to declare that there is "no question" that human activity is the source of rising CO_2 emissions. See "EXXON Shifted on Climate Change Under Trump Pick," *The Hill*, December 16, 2016, *http://thehill.clm/policy/energy-environment /310647-exxon-shifted-on-climate-change-undeer-trump-pick*.

37. Reported in "News: Colombia," *The Tablet*, September 16, 2017, 24.

38. Michael Shear, "Trump Will Withdraw U.S. From Paris Climate Agreement," *New York Times*, June 1, 2017, *www.nytimes.com/2017/06/01/climate/trump-paris -climate-agreement.html*. The United States is the only member state at the Paris agreement that is withdrawing; recently Syria and Nicaragua signed on.

The Responses

The strongest sign that the world's leaders take climate change seriously is still the Paris Agreement, adopted by 195 countries in Paris on December 12, 2015, signed by 193 countries by November 2016, and ratified by 116 nations. The agreement, which went into force on November 4, 2016, aims to limit the rise in global average temperature to two degrees Celsius above preindustrial levels. The agreement is voluntary with no enforcement mechanism. However, it does serve as a wakeup call.[39] Even with the withdrawal by the United States, the agreement seems to be gaining strength. Note that of three holdouts after 2015, the United States, Syria, and Nicaragua, both Syria and Nicaragua signed in 2017. Thus by its withdrawal the United States is the lone holdout.

In addition, the signatories to the Agreement have vowed to push on with their commitments on curbing emissions to reduce

World leaders signed the Paris climate agreement in 2016. U.S. Secretary of State John Kerry (seated), one of the leaders in bringing more than 150 nations together, signs for the United States. In 2018, President Donald Trump withdrew the United States from the agreement.

---

39. "What Will Happen If America's President-Elect Follows through on Pledges to Tear Up Environmental Laws?" *Economist*, November 26, 2016, 55–57, *www.economist.com/news/international/21710811-rest-world-will-figure-out-way-stay-course-what-will-happen-if-americas*.

global warming and the ill effects of climate change. Christiana Figueres, executive director of the UN Framework Convention on Climate Change (UNFCCC), who led the negotiations on the Paris Agreement among 195 nations, wrote that she "was moved to thank the president" because "Trump's announcement provoked an unparalleled wave of support for the treaty. He shored up the world's resolve on climate action."[40]

Noting the support in the United States around such efforts as California's plans for a Climate Action Summit for September 2018, the strong continuing support from developing nations, island states, and indigenous peoples, Figueres is optimistic. "It is my conviction that—far from being embattled—our movement has become more participatory, more invigorated, and more democratic than ever before."[41]

As if to underscore Figueres's view, Mark Tercek, president and CEO of the Nature Conservancy, notes that in the United States alone more than "1,200 universities, colleges, investors, businesses, mayors, and governors recently sent a letter to the United Nations underscoring their pledge to help the U.S. make good on its promise for climate action."[42]

Catholic Social Teaching: Justice for People and the Planet

Catholic social teaching (CST) addresses climate change and advocates for justice for Earth and its people and other life forms in two ways.

First, principles such as worker justice and the common good as articulated in early CST documents become the building blocks for later developments throughout the teachings. For example, the preferential option for the poor now relates to those most harmed

---

40. Christiana Figueres, "We'll Always Have Paris," *Sierra Magazine*, November/ December 2017, 34.

41. Ibid., 35. For additional responses from Figueres, see Fiona Harvey, "World Has 3 Years Left to Stop Dangerous Climate Change," *The Guardian*, June 28 2017.

42. Mark Tercek, "A Consensus Climate Solution," blog, June 20, 2017, *https:// blog.naature.org/conservancy/2017/06/20/a-consensus-climate-solution/?intc3 =nature-climate-lp.splash2.*

by climate change—poor, vulnerable, and marginalized peoples impacted by the structural violence related to climate change.[43] They are harmed by flooding of the low-lying areas where many live, salinization of their farmlands as seawaters move inland and upstream in rivers, more severe weather patterns, and less water for irrigation. The preferential option now calls for needs of impoverished people and the impoverished Earth itself to receive priority.

Second, the foundation of CST's ethical analysis, namely, the common good, now becomes the universal common good, relevant to all, from the poor to the wealthy and to Earth—all are threatened by climate change, but especially the poor.

US Bishops and Catholic Communities

In its 1991 pastoral statement, *Renewing the Earth*, the US Conference of Catholic Bishops (USCCB) addressed climate change as a moral issue. The degradation of the planet harmed poor and marginalized communities in particular. Their concerns were addressed again in 2001 when they published "Global Climate Change: A Plea for Dialogue and the Common Good." Then on November 16, 2017, the leaders of some 161 Catholic organizations—colleges and universities, religious communities, national Catholic organizations, health care providers—issued a letter to President Trump and Congress supporting climate change science and asking for continued funding of the UN Framework Convention on Climate Change. As Bishop Richard Pates of Des Moines noted: "Catholic concern for climate change as a moral issue goes back to Pope John Paul II."[44]

---

43. To underscore this point see Shiva, *Water Wars*, xxix-xxi, for examples of violence and water issues today.

44. USCCB, *Renewing the Earth*, November 14, 1991, *www.usccb.org/issues-and -action/human-life-and-dignity/environment/renewing-the-earth.cfm*; USCCB, "Global Climate Change: A Plea for Dialogue and the Common Good," June 15, 2001, *www .usccb.org/issues-and-action/human-life-and-dignity/environment/global-climate-change -a-plea-for-dialogue-prudence-and-the-common-good.cfm*; Catholic Climate Covenant, "U.S. Catholic Community Delivers Climate Change Letter to President Trump and Congress," November 16, 2017, *www.catholicclimatecovenant.org/press-release/u-s -catholic-community-delivers-climate-change-letter-to-president-trump-and -congress?eType=EmailBlastContent&eId=ba0d58a1-3acd-42eb-8a1a-d996debb187b.*

Vatican Responses

Pope Benedict XVI

Benedict XVI addressed climate change in his 2007 letter to Orthodox Patriarch Bartholomew I: "Protection of the environment, and particular attention to climate change are matters of grave concern for the entire human family."[45] Then in his 2009 encyclical, *Caritas in veritate* (*Charity in Truth*), he continued that thrust: "*The protection* of the environment and of the climate obliges all international leaders to show a readiness to work in good faith, respecting the law and promoting solidarity with the weakest regions of the planet" (*CV* 50). Here, he describes the close link between harm to the environment and harm to people: "Every violation of solidarity and civic friendship harms the environment, just as environmental deterioration in turn upsets relations in society" (*CV* 51).

Benedict XVI addresses a tendency to reduce God's gifts in nature, and thus water, to commodities: "Reducing nature merely to a collection of contingent data ends up doing violence to the environment" (*CV* 48). Furthermore, hoarding energy resources by wealthier states and stockpiling natural resources, "which in many cases are found in the poor countries themselves, gives rise to exploitation" (*CV* 49)—a reference to the structural dimension of climate change's violence to poor communities and countries.[46]

Pope Francis: Climate Change Is Structural Violence

Pope Francis's argument in *Laudato si': On Care for Our Common Home* (2015) is based on the premise that Earth's climate is a common good (*LS* 23), belonging to all people (*LS* 174).

---

45. Benedict XVI, "Letter to Bartholomew I, Ecumenical Patriarch of Constantinople," September 1, 2007, *https://w2.vatican.va/content/benedict-xvi/en/letters/2007/documents/hf_ben-xvi_let_20070901_symposium-environment.html*. Quoted in John Sniegocki, "The Political Economy of Sustainability," in Christiana Z. Peppard and Andrea Vicini, eds., *Just Sustainability* (Maryknoll, NY: Orbis, 2015), 65–66.

46. For further discussion of CST and climate change, in particular Pope Benedict XVI's positions, see John Brinkman, "Discernment of the Church and the Dynamics of the Climate Change Convention," chapter 10 in James Schaefer and Tobias Winright, *Environmental Justice and Climate Change* (Plymouth, UK; Plymouth Publishing, 2013).

In the coming decades, the worst impacts of climate change will be felt in developing countries. Many poor people live in areas particularly affected by phenomena related to warming, as discussed previously, and their means of subsistence are at risk (*LS* 25). Throughout the encyclical, Francis links oppression of Earth with the plight of the poor, a link that Catholic ethicist Kevin O'Brien refers to when he calls climate change structural violence.[47]

The introduction to Francis's encyclical outlines the nature of the violence to nature and poor people when he notes that Earth "cries out to us because of the harm we have inflicted on her by our irresponsible use and abuse of the goods" of creation. "The violence present in our hearts, wounded by sin, is also reflected in the symptoms of sickness, evident in the soil, in the water, in the air and in all forms of life" (*LS* 2). The fault here lies in the structures of exploitation of the goods of creation to serve particular interests. Sin "is manifest in all its destructive power in . . . the abandonment of the most vulnerable, and attacks on nature" (*LS* 66). Francis is framing the "care of the commons" in strong moral terms.

Climate change is rooted in the structures of production and consumption used internationally (*LS* 26). Given the place Francis attaches to human responsibility for creating these problems, he frames the issue of climate change in ethical principles of the common good, the dignity of persons, solidarity, and the preferential option for the poor, now including the poor Earth, into a cohesive whole of "ecological integrity." People and Earth are linked in solidarity. At the heart of the analysis lies the consumptive lifestyle of wealthy and powerful countries and people: "a world of exacerbated consumption is at the same time a world which mistreats life in all its forms" (*LS* 230).

In an evaluation of *Laudato si'*, Brigitte Knopf, secretary general of the Mercator Research Institute on Global Commons and Climate Change (MCC), writes that "with his encyclical, *Laudato si'*, the Pope has presented a pioneering political analysis with great explosive power, which will probably determine the public debate on climate change, poverty and inequality for years to come."[48]

---

47. Kevin O'Brien, "Christian Nonviolence as a Response to Climate Change," presented at Just Sustainability conference, Seattle University, August 4–6, 2016.

48. Brigitte Knopf, "Heaven Belongs to Us All—The New Papal Encyclical," *Real Climate*, June 18, 2015, *www.mcc-berlin.net/en/institute/team/knopf-brigitte.html.* Knopf is also coeditor of *Climate Change, Justice, and Sustainability* (Springer: New York, 2012).

In early 2017, building on Francis's groundbreaking encyclical with its key discussion of climate change, the USCCB along with Catholic Relief Services (CRS) addressed a letter to former Secretary of State Rex Tillerson, noting the importance of Francis's encyclical: "By presenting the care for creation from an ethical and moral standpoint, the Pope has invited all to rise above these unhelpful divisions. We have one common home, and we must protect it."[49]

The US bishops also expressed their dismay upon learning of President Trump's decision to withdraw from the Paris climate agreement. Bishop Oscar Cantu, chair of the Bishops' Committee on International Justice and Peace wrote that, "The Scriptures affirm the value of caring for creation and caring for each other in solidarity," and that, "the Paris agreement is an international accord that promotes these values." In strong words Bishop Cantu wrote that the USCCB, Pope Francis and "the entire Catholic Church have consistently upheld the Paris Agreement as an important international mechanism to promote environmental stewardship and encourage climate change mitigation."[50]

Meanwhile Pope Francis in his address on World Food Day, October 16, 2017,[51] called upon nations to work collectively on issues of climate change and hunger and the refugee crisis, all related. "We see consequences of climate change every day," he said. "Thanks to scientific knowledge, we know how we have to confront the problem and the international community has also worked out the legal methods, such as the Paris Accord, which sadly, some have abandoned," a direct reference to the Trump administration's decision to withdraw from the agreement. "How do you stop people who are ready to risk everything, entire generations that can disappear for

---

49. Michael Hill for CRS and USCCB, "CRS and Catholic Bishops Call on Administration to Address Climate Change," February 18, 2017, www.crs.org/media-center/news-release/crs-and-catholic-bishops-call-administration-address-climate-change.

50. Vatican Radio, Sean Patrick Lovett, "American Bishops Decry Trump's Decision on Climate Change," June 2, 2017, http://en.radiovaticana.va/news/2017/06/02/american_bishops_decry_trumps_decision_on_climate_change/1316436. Bishops from around the world have emphasized the moral issues involved in climate change, from Ireland, to Canada, and Peru, www.catholicclimatecovenant.org/teachings/globalbishops.

51. The UN Food and Agricultural Organization celebrates World Food Day each year on October 16, commemorating the organization's founding in 1945. More than 150 countries participate in events, www.fao.org/world-food-day/2017/about/en/.

lack of their daily bread, or because they are the victims of violence or climate change?"[52]

Conclusion

Earth's atmosphere is warming, with dramatic and harmful impacts on humans, other life forms, and Earth. Whether in the form of former islands submerged beneath the ocean, more frequent and severe weather events, disappearing polar ice caps, or dead or dying coral reefs, the dangers will continue. In spite of the US president's policy to withdraw from the Paris climate agreement, the agreement, is a hopeful sign. However, these signs of danger and hope need strong and articulate ethical advocates.

Drawing on rich principles of CST, Pope Francis delivers an argument beyond technological and even political solutions. He argues that the climate crisis is "one small sign of the ethical, cultural and spiritual crisis of modernity" (*LS* 119), a modernity "grounded in a utilitarian mindset" (*LS* 210). He calls then for ecological conversion and education about not only climate change but also the variety of threats to the global commons. While the costs of meeting the challenges brought about by climate change are tremendous, Francis reminds us that decisions made "are primarily ethical decisions, rooted in solidarity between all peoples" (*LS* 172).

Review Questions

1. What does the term *climate change* mean?
2. What evidence is there that climate change is taking place?
3. What evidence is there that humans cause climate change?
4. What are some effects of climate change?
5. How has CST responded to climate change? Is the response strong enough? Explain.

---

52. Jessica Corbett, "For Abandoning Climate Accord, Pope Swipes Trump on World Food Day," *https://www.commondreams.org/news/2017/10/16/abandoning-climate-accord-pope-swipes-trump-world-food-day*.

6. How would you strengthen the moral/ethical argument about climate change?
7. Which principle of CST is the most important to you in addressing climate change?

Discussion Questions

1. In conversation with another student, what evidence could you present that there is a human cause to climate change?
2. What are the arguments of deniers/skeptics that climate change is or is not human caused? How would you strengthen or refute those arguments?
3. Does climate change impact you now? In what ways?
4. How might climate change impact you in the future? What if you lived on an island? What if you lived inland?

CHAPTER

A Polluted Earth in the Twenty-first Century

The story of the water crisis in Flint, Michigan, may have begun when General Motors left the city, taking hundreds of well-paid jobs with it. Back then, the water was still good. Maybe the crisis began when Flint became a largely African American city of low-income residents with a 40 percent poverty rate.[1] Yet still, the water was fine. Some might say it began when Flint filed for bankruptcy, and the governor appointed a nonresident city manager, leaving citizens with no elected voices to speak for them. At that time, the water was still good.

In April 2014, to save money, the city manager switched the city's water supply from the nearby Detroit River to the polluted Flint River. Immediately, citizens noticed their drinking water looked different, tasted poor, and smelled bad. After drinking the water and bathing and washing in it, they reported skin rashes and expressed concern about bacteria. The unelected city manager replied, "Flint water is safe to drink."[2] By August 2014, coliform bacteria were detected. In response, city officials advised residents to boil their water.[3]

---

1. Michael Martinez, "Flint, Michigan: Did Race and Poverty Factor into Water Crisis?," CNN, *www.cnn.com/2016/01/26/us/flint-michigan-water-crisis-race-poverty/index.html*.

2. Jeremy Lin, Jean Rutter, and Haeyoun Park, "Events That Led to Flint's Water Crisis," *New York Times*, January 21, 2014, *www. nytimes.com/interactive/2016/01/21/US/flint-lead-water-timeline.html*.

3. Ibid.

In January 2015, Detroit city managers offered to reconnect the Detroit River water system to Flint, but Flint's emergency manager turned them down. Then in February 2015, citizen Lee Anne Walters discovered there were 104 parts per billion of lead in her drinking water, far beyond the federal safety level of 15 parts per billion. She notified the Environmental Protection Agency (EPA). No action was taken. By March, a second testing at her home detected 397 parts per billion of lead.

In late September, Mona Hanna-Attisha, MD, of Hurley Medical Center in Flint, along with other doctors, found high levels of lead in the blood of many Flint children. They urged the city to stop using water from the Flint River. State regulators assured citizens that the water was safe. Flint reconnected to the Detroit River water system, but residents were still advised to use filtered water.

It wasn't until December 14, 2015, that the city declared an emergency. On January 5, 2016, Governor Rick Snyder declared a state of emergency for Genesse County, which includes Flint; and on January 16, 2016, President Barack Obama declared a state of emergency over the polluted, unsafe water in the city and surrounding county, which allowed the Federal Emergency Management Agency (FEMA) to provide aid up to $5 million.[4]

In April 2016, on the day before Earth Day, a *New York Times* editorial praised the announcement that Michigan's attorney general, Bill Schuette, had filed criminal charges against three officials, Flint's utilities manager and two state Department of Environmental Quality officers, accusing them of "felonies and misdemeanors, including misconduct in office and tampering with evidence." The editorial board said,

> It is important that the investigation continue not only to hold people accountable, but also to help restore faith in the government of Michigan and the Environmental Protection Agency. Both have betrayed the city and its residents. Officials lied about what they were doing. The E.P.A. was unconscionably slow to intervene.[5]

---

4. Ibid.

5. Editorial Board, "Seeking Justice for Flint Residents," *New York Times*, April 21, 2016, A26.

Tainted and toxic tap water similar to the tap water that Flint, Michigan, residents experienced daily. How does a resident boil this water until it is "clean"?

By the end of 2016, eleven officials, from the local to state level, were charged with offenses, including "false pretenses and conspiracy to commit false pretenses," and "misconduct in office and willful neglect of duty." In late December 2016, residents were still being advised to not drink tap water without filters. Wary of "official" statements, many residents relied on bottled water.[6]

This situation continues to harm and endanger not only the physical health of the citizens of Flint but also their mental health and dignity, an additional suffering to poor residents. The tap water of Flint as reported by resident Janice Berryman had extremely high levels of lead as late as February 2016, and family members, in fear, had stopped visiting.

Bob and Johanna Atwood Brown installed faucet filters and bought bottled water for drinking. However, for cooking or making coffee or Kool-Aid for their ten-year-old son and his friends, they used filtered tap water. By January 2016, their water tested with lead at 200 parts per billion—more than could be filtered out and more than the federal safety level of 15 parts per billion. Johanna Brown said, "The guilt is unreal. I poisoned other

6. Monica Davey and Mitch Smith, "Two Former Flint Emergency Managers Are Charged Over Tainted Water," *New York Times*, December 21, 2016, A12, 14.

people's children. . . . Are we going to get cancer from this? I'm terrified."[7]

Like Janice Berryman and the Browns, many Flint residents have experienced fear, guilt, stress, depression, anger, and even breakdowns or suicidal feelings because of their toxic drinking water.[8] Two years later, a study by Daniel Grossman of West Virginia University and David Slusky of the University of Kansas revealed that in the year following the change of water supplier, "the number of births per woman aged fifteen to forty-nine fell by 15 percent compared with the average over the previous eight years, while fetal deaths increased." They noted that their data do not include abortions and miscarriages that occur in the first twenty weeks of pregnancy. The authors concluded that "[it] may take decades for all the consequences of Flint's water crisis to become known."[9] This is a heavy mental burden for Flint residents to carry.

The city of Flint, Michigan, is now synonymous with criminal government negligence at the local, state, and national levels; institutional racism directed against a minority group largely living in poverty; and lack of political will to carry out needed reforms. The water crisis in Flint illustrates a flagrant lack of attention to basic principles and practices of justice, a negligence devoid of any sense of the common good, accountability, citizen participation, and fundamental human dignity with particular emphasis on the poor and vulnerable. The Flint debacle raises important ethical questions: "Who was responsible? How did it happen?"[10]

Water Pollution: An Ancient Yet Contemporary Crisis

The Flint story is but one of countless cases worldwide of human-caused pollution. For example, in the summer of 2015, a water

---

7. Abby Goodnough and Scott Atkinson, "Flint Water Crisis Also Hits at Mental Health," *New York Times*, May 1, 2016, A1.

8. Ibid.

9. The Data Team, "The Water Crisis in Flint, Michigan Has Had Terrible Consequences for Residents' Health," *The Economist*, September 27, 2017, *www.economist.com/blogs/graphicdetail/2017/09/daily-chart-18*.

10. See chapter 6, "Selling Water: Privatization of a Scarce Resource," in this book for further discussion of Flint and bottled water.

pollution crisis surprised residents of Silverton, Colorado, a small former mining town in the southwestern part of the state. The shuttered Gold King Mine, ten miles north, housed an acidic, metal-laden pool of water deep inside, a leftover from decades of mining. The pool sought escape from its dank prison and on August 5, found release.

Outside the mine, an excavator had worked its way around the debris on the mine's slope while contractors and employees of the Environmental Protection Agency watched, unaware of the brew building up inside. All summer the crew had been putting in bulkheads to control the toxic water draining from the tunnels. Due to the danger involved, the on-site EPA coordinator had paused the work, but while he was on vacation; his replacement decided to proceed. Then by 10:30 a.m., August 5, a thin stream began flowing from the old mine, which quickly grew into a fountain and then to a waterfall of orange water, of what is known as "acid mine drainage."

Acid mine drainage is a complicated outcome of mining processes. First, snow, rainwater, and groundwater seep naturally through the cracks and openings in the ground above and around the mine. The mine tunnels, however, intercept the water and expose it to oxygen and pyrite. That in turn results in a chemical reaction that produces the acid mine mixture. "When these two [pyrite and oxygen] collide, oxygen rusts the iron in the pyrite, yielding orange iron oxides." The process is almost impossible to stop.[11] The resultant bonding creates sulfuric acid, dissolving zinc, cadmium, lead, copper, aluminum, arsenic and other metals—a toxic brew, rendering streams deadly to fish and other aquatic life forms.

So when the Gold King Mine wastewater rushed over the edge of the mine's dump,[12] the torrent, filled with tons of metal-laden material, crashed into the small stream of North Fork Cement Creek. Swirling down the mountainside. In another six miles the swollen creek blasted into the Animas River at Silverton. Twenty-four hours later, the poisoned river water reached the steep gorge

---

11. Jonathan Thompson, "Silverton's Gold King Reckoning," *High Country News*, May 2, 2016, 10–17; Jonathan Thompson, "Chemistry 101 on the Animas," *High Country News*, September 14, 2015, 3.

12. The dump is the site where the mine's refuse, including toxic water, is stored.

below Silverton and cascaded into the Animas River valley just a few miles upstream from Durango, Colorado, near the border with New Mexico.

Long time Durango resident Jonathan Thompson described the scene: "Turbid, electric-orange water, utterly opaque, sprawled out between the sandy banks, as iron hydroxide particles thickened with the current, like psychedelic smoke." Irrigation intakes shuttered for 100 miles along the river as the flow continued past Durango toward the San Juan River and northwestern border areas of New Mexico. The small fields of the Navajo Nation along the San Juan River were especially hard hit.

In May 2016, New Mexico sued the EPA and the mine's owners for damages caused by these events. The suit claims the spill "wrought environmental and economic damage" as the Animas River flowed into the state.[13] The real cause of the Gold King Mine spill remains "Colorado's legacy of abandoned metal mines with no culpable owners."[14] However, on Monday, June 26, 2017, the US Supreme Court rejected New Mexico's lawsuit against Colorado that claimed that negligence by Colorado environmental regulators played a direct role in the spill of more than 3 million gallons of mine waste and so brought about an environmental disaster that polluted the San Juan and Animas rivers in New Mexico. The legal arguments continue as New Mexico now pursues a suit against the federal government and the mine's original owners in lower federal court.[15]

Water Pollution: United States and Worldwide

Water pollution results from waste from heavy industry and domestic processes; semitreated wastewater; runoff from agricultural, business, and residential use of fertilizers and pesticides; waste from boats and ships; and leaking septic tanks, among other sources. Hundreds of gallons of untreated wastewater find their way into fresh and

---

13. Jonathan Thompson, "New Mexico Sues over Orange River," *High Country News*, June 13, 2016, 3.

14. Dennis Wentz, "Letter," *High Country News*, October 26, 2015, 4.

15. Andrew Oxford, "Supreme Court Dismisses N.M. Suit against Colorado over Mine Spill," *The New Mexican*, June 26, 2017.

salt water around the world. In the United States, more than eight hundred cities collect overflow rainwater and human and industrial sewage in the same pipes; so overflow does not go to treatment plants but into rivers and streams.[16] The Colorado River contains a noxious brew of pesticides, mercury, flame retardants, and other poisons that have resulted in an "unacceptable risk" to humans and the environment.[17]

Water quality is also dangerous in other parts of the world. Three-fourths of the rivers in Poland are unfit for use, even by industry, due to chemicals, sewage, and agricultural run-off. In Latin America, 98 percent of domestic sewage flows raw into natural water bodies. Worldwide, 90 percent of people still drop their bodily wastes and sewage into natural water bodies.[18] In the Middle East, the Jordan River, which flows through Israel, Jordan, and the Palestinian territories, including the West Bank, is so polluted that regional environmentalists are calling for an end to baptisms in its waters.[19] New Zealand's concerns involve the huge amounts of excrement and urine from its dairy cattle industries. Despite efforts to fence streams off from cattle, streams and lakes are infiltrated with algae blooms. Chemicals from feces also work their ways into aquifers needed for drinking water in some places.[20]

Toxic industrial pollutants, such as PCBs, dioxin, mercury, lead, and many others, often come from industries discharging their effluents directly into natural water bodies. Mercury pollution has been documented around the world. Just 0.07ml[21] of mercury can pollute a lake with a twenty-acre surface area to the point that its fish are unsafe to eat.[22]

Rivers in the former Soviet Union are heavily contaminated from agricultural runoff, industrial waste, radioactive waste, and

---

16. De Villiers, *Water*, 89.

17. "Notes," *High Country News*, February 16, 2009, 5.

18. Maggie Black, *The No-nonsense Guide to Water* (London: Verso, 2004), 23–25, 45.

19. "Up to Speed," *Sierra Magazine*, November–December 2010, 21.

20. Banyan, "A Clean and Pleasant Land," *The Economist*, September 23, 2017, 38.

21. One-seventieth of a teaspoon.

22. Dashka Slater, "This Much Mercury Can Contaminate a 20-acre Lake," *Sierra Magazine*, November–December 2011, 50.

bacteria from human daily uses. Even in Western Europe, water pollution is "severe." In Ireland, for example, 30 percent of the rivers are heavily polluted; in Britain, more than four thousand rivers are likewise polluted.[23] More than half of the world's rivers pose severe health problems to those living near them.[24]

Contaminants that flow from human bodies and daily, personal actions are a key source of water pollution. Humans bathe, wash, rinse, shave, brush their teeth, use creams and lotions, drink coffee and alcohol, take medicines, which make their way into waters. Indeed, researchers have documented drugs such as Prozac, caffeine, cholesterol medicine, ibuprofen, and more in wastewater and in the tissue of juvenile Chinook salmon in Washington's Puget Sound.[25]

Oceans

In addition to the increasingly warm and acidic oceans caused by carbon dioxide emissions and climate change, discussed in chapter 2, pollution from agriculture, businesses, homes, and other sources have created more than 408 "dead zones" in the ocean—areas at or near the bottom of the ocean without sufficient oxygen to support fish or other marine life. Most are close to the coastlines of northern countries, such as the United States, Japan, and many European countries. One of the largest dead zones is in the Gulf of Mexico, fed by pesticides and fertilizers from agricultural and other runoffs that flow into the Mississippi River. By October 2017, the Gulf's dead zone was the size of New Jersey, the largest size ever.[26] Let's take a closer look at the problems in our oceans caused by pollution.

Sunscreen and Coral, Again

More than six thousand tons of sunscreen wash off swimmers' bodies into the oceans each year. The mix of UV blockers, preservatives,

23. Sean McDonagh, *Dying for Water* (Dublin: Veritas Publications, 2003), 27, 41.

24. De Villiers, *Water*, 87–89.

25. "Drugs in Puget Sound Salmon," *PCC Sound Consumer: News Bites*, July 2016, 11.

26. "Up to Speed," *Sierra Magazine*, November–December 2017, 20.

coloring agents, fragrances, spreading agents, and surfactants "play havoc with marine ecosystems" and cause "coral reef bleaching and die-off."[27] The equivalent of a drop of sunscreen in a body of water the size of six Olympic-sized swimming pools is enough to damage the delicate organisms in coral.[28] Hit by chemicals, corals expel algae and lose their vibrant colors. Bleaching kills coral, causing coral reefs to degrade, no longer providing important habitat for fish or other marine life or no longer offering protection from storm surges or hurricanes for coastal communities.

Snorkeling is one way sunscreen makes its way to coral reefs. A 2016 article in the *Sound Consumer* reported that in high-tourist areas, the oil slick from swimmers is a key contributing factor to bleaching. Even far away from coastal areas, people wearing sunscreen head home and take a shower; the washed-off sunscreen makes its way into waste-water, which often reaches the ocean and its coral habitats.[29]

Plastics

The daily routines of many, if not most, people now depend on plastic products—from cell phones to defibrillators to airplanes. In the oceans, however, plastics are deadly. Seabirds, seals, sea lions, turtles, fish, whales, and dolphins think plastics are food and eat them but are unable to digest them. A Plymouth University study revealed that more than seven hundred marine species are affected because they ingest the plastic particles, and estimates suggest more than one hundred million marine mammals die as a result of ingesting plastic pollution or becoming entangled in plastic materials.[30]

For example, tons of the plastic trash dumped in the ocean ends up each year on the Midway Atoll, a cluster of islands in the mid-Pacific Ocean, where the trash harms and often kills the islands' animals. One

---

27. Dashka Slater, "On the Other . . . ," *Sierra Magazine*, July-August 2014, 19. The main culprit is oxybenzone, a chemical found in more than 3,500 sunscreens worldwide.

28. Ibid.

29. Laura Brady, "Sunscreen and Coral Reefs," *Sound Consumer*, July 2016, *www.pccnatural//markets.com/sc/1607/sunscreen-and-coral-reefs.html.*

30. Corrine Henn, "These 5 Marine Animals Are Dying Because of Our Plastic Trash . . . Here's How We Can Help," *One Green Planet*, February 5, 2017, *www.onegreenplanet.org/animalsandnature/marine-animals-are-dying-because-of-our-plastic-trash/.*

of the five major oceanic currents filled with plastics, the North Pacific Gyre, carries the plastic trash to the islands. Some fifty tons of plastic arrive on the shores of the Midway Atoll islands each year.[31]

Ocean and freshwater pollution are not just an environmental concern, but also are societal issues centered on problems of environmental racism and poverty. A return to the Flint story will help to illustrate.

CST in Action: Back to Flint

Water pollution worldwide harms not only ecosystems but also people and communities. This pollution also reflects social, economic, and political ills, such as poverty and marginalization of populations most victimized by pollution. Another look at the Flint story illustrates how water pollution raises ethical concerns around racism and poverty. As Flint resident Sabrina Hernandez, a nineteen-year-old bartender, said, "It makes you think, was this [the water crisis in Flint] because we were poor? . . . Nobody listens to the poor people that are barely making it." Even when Flint was using Detroit's water, the Detroit utility was "charging one of the poorest cities in the United States an average of $910 a year per household, nearly three times the national average."[32]

Today, Flint, which has a population of one hundred thousand, is largely an African American community. If Flint were largely a white community, would officials have ignored the situation for so long? Would an unelected city manager have been allowed to decide the city's fate? Were the troubles in Flint a confluence of poverty, racism, and lack of participation?

Poverty

Communities with large numbers of people living below the poverty line are frequently also the locations chosen for waste

---

31. Elizabeth Shogren, "Remote Waters Offer No Refuge from Plastic Trash," *All Things Considered*, Public Broadcasting System, October 1, 2007, *www.npr.org/templates /story/story.php?storyId=14859155*. The documentary *A Plastic Ocean*, directed by Craig Leeson (January 2017), highlights, among other things, the plight of albatross chicks on Midway that ingest plastics and do not survive, *www.tugg.com/titles/a-plastic-ocean*.

32. Charlie Leduff, "Corroded Trust," *Mother Jones*, May-June, 2016, 8, 9, 11.

dumps, incinerators, and other undesirable by-products of consumer society—by-products that pollute nearby water sources. People in these communities often lack the organizing skills, education, free time, and public voice to challenge powerful political and economic interests. Their voices are drowned out by power and wealth—by cries of, "Not in my backyard!" or NIMBY! from wealthier communities.[33]

Several CST documents and statements by US bishops address these issues of poverty and racism directly. Pope Paul VI stated in his 1971 letter, *Octogesima adveniens* (*A Call to Action*): "the Gospel instructs us in the preferential respect due the poor and the special situation they have in society" (*OA* 23). Around the world, this principle is key to alleviating water shortages in poor communities, particularly in those cases in which women and children walk long distances to secure safe drinking water for their families.

In their 1986 letter, *Economic Justice for All* (*EJA*), the bishops of the United States declared, "The fulfillment of the basic needs of the poor is of the highest priority" in looking at the nation's wealth (*EJA* Intro, 19).[34] The bishops followed this discussion with a focus on pollution and poverty in their 1991 statement, *Renewing the Earth*: "in most countries today, including our own, it is the poor and the powerless who most directly bear the burden of current environmental carelessness. Their lands and neighborhoods are more likely to be polluted or to host toxic waste dumps, their water to be undrinkable."[35]

Racism

A second element in the Flint story is subtle and insidious racism. According to the *New York Times* Editorial Board an independent task force commissioned by Michigan Governor Rick Snyder to

---

33. Manuel Pastor, "Environmental Inequity in Metropolitan Los Angeles," in Robert Bullard, *The Quest for Environmental Justice* (San Francisco: Sierra Club Books, 2005), 117–18. See also Robert Bullard, *The Quest for Environmental Justice* (San Francisco: Sierra Club Books, 2005), 4.

34. Quotes from *EJA* are from *Economic Justice for All: Pastoral Letter on Catholic Social Teaching and the US Economy* (Washington, DC: USCCB, 2009).

35. *Renewing the Earth: An Invitation to Reflection and Action on Environment in Light of Catholic Social Teaching* (Washington, DC: United States Catholic Conference, 1992).

investigate Flint's water crisis tells, without using the term *racism*, the central role of race, as well as poverty: "Flint residents, who are majority black or African-American and among the most impoverished of any metropolitan area in the United States, did not enjoy the same degree of protection from environmental and health hazards as that provided to other communities." When the governor was asked whether race was an issue in the Flint disaster, he said he did not know, "even though the record shows that the concerns of poor and minority residents were dismissed by his administration in ways that would never have happened with rich white communities."[36]

The term *environmental racism* was coined in a study by the United Church of Christ in the 1980s. The study was the first to point out that communities of color too often became America's sites for landfills or polluting industries, such as oil refineries or manufacturing plants. The results in these communities are deadly, ranging from increased rates of asthma to higher incidences of cancer. Robert Bullard, director of the Environmental Justice Resource Center at Clark Atlanta University, put it succinctly: "Environmental racism is a human rights issue. Environmental racism also exacerbates poverty and threatens public health."[37]

Racism is condemned in several papal documents. In the United States, the Catholic Bishops stated, unequivocally, in 1979, "Racism is a radical evil. To struggle against it demands an equally radical transformation, in our own minds and hearts as well as in the structure of our society."[38] In 2015, the Pontifical Council for Justice and Peace wrote, "racism still exists. It is a wound in humanity's side that mysteriously remains open."[39]

---

36. Editorial Board, "The Racism at the Heart of Flint's Crisis," *New York Times*, March 25, 2016, *www.nytimes.com/2016/03/25/opinion/the-racism-at-the-heart-of-flints-crisis.html*.

37. Robert Bullard, *The Quest for Environmental Justice* (San Francisco: Sierra Club Books, 2005), 207.

38. US Conference of Catholic Bishops, *Brothers and Sisters to Us: US Bishops' Pastoral Letter on Racism in Our Day* (Washington, DC: US Catholic Conference, 1979), *www.usccb.org/issues-and-action/cultural-diversity/african-american/brothers-and-sisters-to-us.cfm*.

39. Pontifical Council for Justice and Peace, "Racism: Confronting the Poison in Our Common Home," January 2016, *www.usccb.org/issues-and-action/human-life-and-dignity/racism/upload/racism-backgrounder.pdf*.

CST in Action: Principals on Global Pollution

Several other principles of CST are involved in considering global pollution. In his 1971 letter, *Octogesima adveniens*, Paul VI enunciated the principles of equality and participation as two key forms of human dignity (*OA* 22). The 1986 document of the US Bishops on the US economy, *Economic Justice for All*, states, "Basic justice demands the establishment of minimum levels of participation in the life of the human community for all persons" (*EJA* 77).

The lack of participation by community members in decisions about water that affect the health and welfare of peoples, especially in communities of color and low-income communities, is a striking example of basic injustice. In Flint's case, key leaders failed to include in decision making the very people impacted, and once the governor appointed a manager to make critical decisions about water, the community was no longer able to participate. Another CST principle that applies is subsidiarity, which means that issues should be dealt with at the most local level possible. In Flint, the state acted without local community participation.

Realities surrounding water—in particular threats to health from pollution—are part and parcel of what theologian Christiana Zenner (formerly Peppard), calls the right to life "for the twenty-first century."[40] Certainly, this is true in the literal sense for humans, all other living creatures, and Earth itself.

Another key principle that explores concern about water pollution and human responsibility is the care of creation. Pope John Paul II had long been concerned with humans, relationship to the natural world, from reiterating the principal that "the goods of creation are meant for all" in *Sollicitudo rei socialis* (*SRS* 39) to his 1991 encyclical *Centesimus annus*, in which he links the "irrational destruction of the natural environment" to a rising pattern of consumerism that threatens the fabric of the human environment (*CA* 38).

As noted in chapter 1, the statement of the Vatican's Pontifical Council for Justice and Peace at the 2003 Kyoto World Water Forum paid particular attention to the link between water pollution and poverty: "Many people living in poverty . . . daily face

---

40. Peppard, *Just Water*, 52–67.

enormous hardship because water supplies are neither sufficient nor safe." The key principle supporting this premise is that of solidarity: "The same duty of solidarity that rests on individuals exists also for nations. Advanced nations have a very heavy obligation to help the developing people." In its 2006 letter, the Vatican indicates that "the primary objective of all efforts must be the well-being of those people . . . who suffer most from any scarcity *or misuse* of water resources."[41]

Pope Francis and Water Pollution

In *Laudato si': On Care for Our Common Home*, Francis discusses the relationships among nature ecology, human ecology/economy, and cultural ecology, with a special focus on indigenous populations in their struggles for integrity and against rampant forms of development, pollution, and waste. Francis links poverty of people and poverty of the environment, especially of water, as results of a consumptive society: "Access to safe drinkable water is a basic and universal human right, since it is essential to human survival and, as such, is a condition for the exercise of other human rights. Our world has a grave social debt towards the poor who lack access to drinking water, because they are denied the right to a life consistent with their inalienable dignity" (*LS* 30).

In his discussion of water pollution, Francis argues that pollution is an everyday experience for many (*LS* 28), especially the poor: "Every day, unsafe water results in many deaths and the spread of water-related diseases. Underground water sources are threatened by the pollution produced in certain mining, farming and industrial activities" (*LS* 29).

For Francis, a central theological demand is at work here, namely, that the entire universe finds its destiny in the fullness of the Creator: "The ultimate purpose of other creatures is not to be found in us. Rather, all creatures are moving forward with us and through us towards a common point of arrival, which is God" (*LS* 82). Thus

41. Author's emphasis; Pontifical Council for Justice and Peace, 2006; see the full text of the Council's statement at *www.vatican.va/roman_curia/pontifical_councils /justpeace*.

to misuse those elemental parts is a transgression against the Creator: "The entire material universe speaks of God's love. Soil, water, mountains: everything is, as it were, a caress of God" (*LS* 84). Water pollution strikes at the heart of that divine love.

In Francis's ethical framework, people have a right to water; and humanity owes a social debt to those who lack access to safe drinking water (*LS* 30). Beyond the moral concerns regarding water pollution, the right to water, and the plight of the poor, Francis ties the importance of clean water to water's symbolic purity in relation to the Divine: "Through our worship of God, we are invited to embrace the world on a different plane. Water, oil, fire and colors are taken up in all their symbolic power and incorporated in our act of praise. Water poured over the body of a child in Baptism is a sign of new life" (*LS* 235). If Earth's waters are polluted, how can they symbolize purity and new life with God?

This theological reflection recalls the Canticle of St. Francis that reads, "Praised be you, my Lord, through Sister Water," Sister Water as a symbol of the Divine. In *Laudato si'*, water has found a moral and theological voice that expresses the outrage of contaminated, polluted water damaging people and all of creation.

Conclusion

This chapter began with the plight of the people of Flint, Michigan, and their polluted water. Flint provides a case study for major CST themes—principles that call for systemic changes in personal and political actions—in which the problem of water pollution is treated at the source, not just in terms of its effects. Francis, especially, puts clean water at the center of his theological and ethical analyses for use as tools in challenging world leaders and individuals to value, respect, and purify water everywhere.

Review Questions

1. What are the main sources of water pollution?
2. What was the cause of water pollution in Flint, Michigan?

3. How did authorities respond to the Flint water crisis?
4. Who is most responsible for Flint's water pollution? Why?
5. How are corals affected by water pollution?

Discussion Questions

1. Identify the reasons why the Flint River became polluted.
2. What water pollution issues are most worrisome? Why?
3. How is racism evident in water pollution issues?
4. Is Pope Francis's response to water pollution adequate? Why or why not?

CHAPTER

Water Scarcity for Most and Abundance for Few

Some people use public goods like water for their private benefit. Lynda and Stewart Resnick love pomegranate juice. They also like almonds[1] and pistachios. Through their California-based company, the Wonderful Company, they tout the health benefits of each, all of which have made the Resnicks a fortune. California's Central Valley is a wonderful place to grow crops, but it has one major problem; the valley sometimes receives an annual rainfall as little as five to sixteen inches. That means water for their crops must come from somewhere else.

Irrigation of the Resnicks' trees consume 117 billion gallons of water a year. Meanwhile, California had experienced a five-year drought. Currently, the Resnicks' company uses more water for irrigation than is used by all of the homes in Los Angeles and the entire San Francisco Bay Area combined.[2] In 2015, Stewart Resnick announced that, by 2020, he would increase his farm's nut acreage by 40 percent. That increase would require a lot of water.

Where would the billions of gallons more of water come from? For that large a number, rainfall is just "a drop in the bucket."

---

1. The almond industry is California's third agricultural crop and was valued at $6.4 billion for 2013. See Almond Board of California, "California Almond Industry Facts," February 2015, *www.almonds.com/pdfs/california-almond-industry-facts.pdf.*

2. For comparison, Los Angeles area water usage for the month of lowest usage in January 2015 was 12,524 million gallons and for the highest in August 2015 was 14,828 million gallons; San Francisco area for the same periods, January was 1,875 million gallons and August was 2,128 million gallons.

Large-scale drip irrigation system on a California farm. Water is brought from an underground source, like an aquifer, then delivered efficiently to the plant roots rather than sprayed above the plants.

Acquiring that much water requires a number of complex business arrangements among landowners and corporations. Some farmers, like the Resnicks, tap into an underground aquifer[3] known as the Kern Water Bank. The Resnicks have a majority vote on the bank's board; in 2007, their share of the bank amounted to 246 billion gallons—"enough to supply the people of San Francisco for 16 years."[4] Then in 2008 came the drought. The Resnicks are still entitled to their share of the bank's water, and they have built canals connecting their land to state and federal water systems as well as thousands of acres of ponds "capable of sucking important water underground." These efforts secure enough water for the Resnicks at the expense of other water users.

A stark contrast of water inequality exists between the company's abundant use for crops and its workers' access to water. Worker

---

3. An aquifer is an underground layer of water stored in permeable rock and soil from which groundwater can be extracted using a water well, pumps, or other extractive measures. See "Aquifers and Groundwater" at the website of the US Geological Survey's Water Science School, *water.usgs.gov/edu/earthgwaquifer.html*.

4. Josh Harkinson, "Some Kind of Wonderful," *Mother Jones*, May–June, 2016, 33–30.

Rafaela Tijerina and her husband bought 330 acres of wheat fields. Unfortunately, without the funds to drill a well or tap into the local irrigation district, the drought ruined their wheat fields. As Tijerina said, "It's really good land. But, we don't have water." The Resnicks have an abundance of water to grow nuts, but their workers do not have enough to water their own crops.[5] Thus water inequality creates economic inequality.

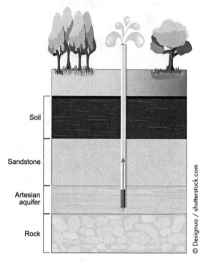

The Resnicks provide perks for their workers, but their workers are among the poorest in the state. In the town of Lost Hills, where most workers live, the Resnicks built a park and an after-school computer lab, and have provided free health clinics with a full-time, bilingual doctor and free prescription medications.

Example of how water is pumped to the surface from an underground source, here from an aquifer, a natural cavern of water filled by surface rainwater. Many aquifers are depleted by heavy withdrawals, unable to refill sufficiently.

These perks for the workers are pennies when compared with the dollars spent by the Resnicks to buy the public water that would otherwise be available to the workers.

Global Scarcity

The story of the Resnicks versus the Tijerinas is one of privileged access to abundant water versus little access to scarce water. It is a story of a wealthy and powerful family using its success to leverage water benefits from the state of California and a family of modest means that is completely dependent on "God's water"—the rain—to meet its needs.

---

5. Harkinson, "Some Kind of Wonderful," 33–30.

Then consider water scarcity that results in little or no water and in unusable, polluted water. The 2015 Joint Monitoring Report of the World Health Organization (WHO) and United Nations Children's Fund (UNICEF) noted that 783 million people do not have access to clean water, and 2.4 billion lack good sanitation.[6] "The impact on child mortality rates is devastating with more than 340,000 children under five who die annually from diarrhoeal diseases due to poor sanitation, poor hygiene, or unsafe drinking water—that is almost 1000 per day."[7]

The United Nations estimates that "By 2025, 1.8 billion people are expected to be living in countries or regions with absolute water scarcity, and two-thirds of the world population could be existing in water-stress conditions."[8] A 2017 UNICEF report especially

Woman searching for water source. Globally, women are primarily responsible for carrying water to the home, sometimes walking miles to find water for the household—enough water for cleaning, bathing, cooking, and so on.

---

6. World Health Organization and UNICEF, *Progress on Drinking Water and Sanitation: 2012 Update*. United States: WHO/UNICEF Joint Monitoring Programme for Water Supply and Sanitation; 2012, *https://www.cdc.gov/healthywater/global/wash_statistics.html*. See also *www.un.org/en/sections/issues-depth/water/*.

7. UN Water, "World Water Development Report 2017," *www.unwater.org/water-facts/water-sanitation-and-hygiene*.

8. UN Water, "Water Scarcity," *www.unwater.org/water-facts/scarcity*.

Example of extreme "desertification." Lack of water causes the land to dry up and fracture.

expresses concerns for the future plight of children in those areas. It predicts that by 2040 approximately 600 million children will live in regions experiencing extreme water stress; the poorest and most disadvantaged will suffer most. Parts of Ethiopia, Nigeria, Somalia, South Sudan, and Yemen will be among the regions especially stressed.[9]

Although climate change and pollution account for some of the predicted water scarcity and water stress felt by peoples and countries, other causes contribute as well, such as poor water management and low pricing, with little incentive to conserve. Given these realities, it is important to examine how freshwater is used today in agriculture, industry, and personal consumption.

---

9. UNICEF, "Thirsting for a Future: Water and Children in Changing Climate," March 22, 2017, *www.unicef.org/wash/waterandclimate.* See also Ben Quinn and Saeed Kalimi Dehghan, "World Water Day: One in Four Children Will Live in Water Scarcity by 2040," *The Guardian,* March 22, 2017, *www.theguardian.com ;global-development/2017/mar/22/world-water-day-one-in-four-children-will-live -with-water-scarcity-by-2040-unicef-report.* For a challenging account of scarcity and abundance, see Vandana Shiva, *Water Wars,* 1–17.

Increase in Demand

Agriculture[10]

Seventy to 80 percent of the world's freshwater is used for irrigation in agriculture. An increasing population means a greater need for agricultural products.[11] Issues about food are directly related to concerns about sufficient supplies of drinking water.

Turfgrass

Perhaps the most surprising crop impacting water supplies is that of turfgrass. Turfgrass is found on lawns, golf courses, business landscapes, city parks, indeed almost everywhere. Turfgrass is the largest irrigated crop in the United States, "occupying three times more land than irrigated cornfields."[12] A 2017 study reveals that, "at the time of this writing, in most regions outdoor water use already reaches 50–75 percent of the total residential use."[13] Water carries the excess nitrogen-rich fertilizer from lawns into streams and oceans, creating an ecological imbalance and "causing algae blooms, degrading water quality, and killing fish."[14]

As urban populations increase and new food industries emerge with water needs, ever greater demands will be made on water for

---

10. In this discussion the term *agriculture* is used to mean "the process by which arable land and crops are cultivated, receive water, bear harvest, and are used by human beings . . . [and] need not be intended directly for human consumption (corn for biofuels)," (Peppard, *Just Water*, 70.) For a full discussion of the history and development of agriculture and twenty-first–century agribusiness, see Peppard, chapter 5, "The Agriculture/Water Nexus," in *Just Water*.

11. United Nations, *Water for People, Water for Life*, 204.

12. Michelle Nijhuis, "The Lure of the Lawn: Can Westerners Get Over Their Romance with Turf?," *High Country News*, August 28, 2006, 8ff.

13. Rob Wile, "The American Lawn Is Now the Largest Single 'Crop' In The U.S.," Huffington Post, August, 17, 2015, *www.huffingtonpost.com/entry /lawn-largest-crop-america_us_55d0dc06e4b07addcb43435d.*

14. Michelle Nijhuis, "The Lure of the Lawn," 10, 12.

agriculture. "At present, nearly 80% of the world's population is exposed to high levels of threat to water security, and the increase of world population will have a significant impact on water usage for food. Under a pessimistic low yield scenario, [it is] estimated that 53 percent more crop water consumption and 38% more land are needed to achieve food production goals in 2050."[15]

Industry

Industrial businesses and power plants are second only to agriculture in freshwater use, at about 20 percent of the total water usage worldwide. Farms generally return water polluted with synthetic fertilizers, pesticides, and herbicides back to Earth; power plants return water that is warm back to Earth; and industrial plants often return water that is polluted with "detergents, hydrocarbons, heavy metals, and toxic organic matter."[16] The United States and Europe have made great strides in reducing water emissions by industry, but elsewhere, many industrial plants discharge untreated wastewater into open waterways, polluting more water.[17]

Industries contributing to water pollution are, in order of impact, food and beverage, paper and pulp, textiles, metals, chemicals, wood, and others.[18] The auto and computer industries are also culprits. For example, it takes 2,800 gallons of water to produce the chips for one personal computer. Building a computer uses more than 700 chemicals, more than half of which are hazardous. That explains why Santa Clara County, California, the center of a high-tech industry, "has over 150 groundwater contamination sites and more Superfund sites than any other county in the nation."[19]

---

15. Noemi Mancosu, Richard Snyder, Gavriil Kyriakakis, and Donatella Spano, "Water Scarcity and Future Challenges for Food Production," *Water* (7), www.mdpi.com/2073-4441/7/3/975/htm.

16. Robert Kandel, *Water from Heaven* (New York: Columbia University Press, 2003), 214.

17. United Nations, *Water for People, Water for Life*, 227; United Nations, *Water: A Shared Responsibility*, 21.

18. United Nations, *Water for People, Water for Life*, 229.

19. B. J. Bergman, "The Hidden Life of Computers," *Sierra Magazine*, July–August 1999, 32. For an update of these figures see "The Hidden Water in Everyday Products," Water Calculator, July 1, 2017, www.watercalculator.org/water-use/the-hidden-water-in-everyday-proucts/?cid=285.

Personal Consumption

The population worldwide has increased by three times since the beginning of the twentieth century, but the demand for water has increased by six times in the same period. A 2015 report indicated that global demand for freshwater would certainly outstrip supply as a result of population growth by the middle of this century, provided current levels of consumption continue.[20]

In her 2011 book *Blue Revolution*, investigative journalist Cynthia Barnett records how much water US citizens use. In the first chapter, "The Illusion of Water Abundance," she emphasizes that people in the United States assume water is plentiful and abundant. Barnett reports that citizens pump daily one million acre-feet (325,851,000,000 US gallons) from the High Plains (or Ogallala) aquifer, a large inland, underground sea beneath eight states in the Midwest (an acre-foot equals 325,851 gallons, or enough water to cover an acre of land—the size of a football field—one foot deep). In what Barnett calls the "Big Gulp," America's total daily water use in 2005 came to 410 billion gallons per day. Finally, for those green turf "crops," we used 19 trillion gallons of water per year.[21] The award for the biggest water user goes to President Donald Trump's estate in Palm Beach, Florida, which during the 2007 Florida drought "gulped an average of 2 million gallons per month for lawns and the estate's 22 bathrooms"; the average monthly bill was $10,000.[22]

Water Wars?

Water has been called "the oil of the 21st century" and termed "blue gold."[23] As nations compete for ever scarcer water supplies, tensions

---

20. Chris Arsenalt, "Global Population Growth Threatens to Outstrip Fresh Water Supply," *Reuters*, March 18, 2015, *www.reuters.com/article/us-global-water-consumption /global-population-growth-threatens-to-outstrip-fresh-water-supply-study-idUSKBN 0ME2B720150318.*

21. Cynthia Barnett's interview with researcher Christinas Melesi, August 5, 2009, reported in Barnett's book, *Blue Revolution*, 11–12.

22. Barnett, *Blue Revolution*, 7, 8, 11, 12.

23. Cf. Maude Barlow and Tony Clark, *Blue Gold: The Fight to Stop the Corporate Theft of the World's Water* (New York: New Press, 2002).

are bound to rise. One of the most contentious water disputes is that between Israel and the Palestinians. When Israel seized the West Bank of the Jordan River during the Six-Day War of 1967, it gained access to the headwaters of the river and to the western aquifer; that seizure increased its water supply by more than 50 percent. Whereas Israelis have built systems for irrigation and use water for lawns, pools, and other consumer uses, Palestinians depend on water trucks to carry this precious natural resource through Israeli border crossings at high prices.[24] Additionally in the West Bank area, Palestinians are forbidden to build new wells and only rarely allowed to repair old ones.[25] In 2016, Palestinians received 73 liters of water per day (about 20 gallons) per person, which is less than the 100-liter (25 gallons) minimum recommended by the World Health Organization.[26]

In the United States, water conflicts roil through the seven western states that depend on the mighty Colorado River. Through interstate and federal water agreements as well as water treaties with Mexico, the once mighty Colorado now delivers almost no water to the sea, producing, instead, a shrinking river delta. Agriculture still consumes the largest portion of the river's water, irrigating the fields in the Imperial Valley of central California. Because Colorado River water is subsidized and cheap, waste through evaporation is rampant, with no incentive to reduce consumption. The total amount of water available from the Colorado is dwindling, and the US Geological Survey sees no end in sight to the declining amount.[27]

Nevada, Arizona, and California each claim they have rights to Colorado River water according to "prior appropriation," that is, whoever uses the water first has a right to the future use of it in an equal amount,[28] regardless of the state of the river. Colorado, Wyoming, Utah, and New Mexico, moreover, argue that the most recent

---

24. Linda Gradstein, "For the World," *National Public Radio*, July 19, 2009.

25. Fred Pearce, *When the Rivers Run Dry: The Defining Crisis of the Twenty-First Century* (Boston: Beacon Press, 2006), 160.

26. "Water in the West Bank," *Economist*, July 30, 2016, 38.

27. Pearce, *When the Rivers Run Dry*, 195–97; Tony Davis, "Ultimate Solution," *High Country News*, November 24, 2008, 14.

28. Philip Ball, *Life's Matrix: A Biography of Water* (Berkeley, CA: University of California Press, 2001), 366.

users of the river should give up their access in a crisis. A Denver newspaper states, "It could stack up as the biggest water war in the West. Arizona could get shut off completely."[29]

The human world is not the only "world" to suffer water scarcity. The animal and plant worlds, not to mention the parched Earth, are also suffering water scarcity. For example, the nearly 3,000-year-old giant sequoias of northern California can withstand forest fires and repel insects that kill other tree species, but these ancient giants need huge amounts of water to survive: "They use more than two tonnes [2,000 kg] a day in summertime. And there are multiple indicators . . . to suggest such volumes could soon be unavailable to them."[30]

More People, Less Water

The World Resources Institute ranks thirty-three countries that will likely experience extreme water stress by 2040. The most severely stressed are in the Middle East, namely Bahrain, Kuwait, Palestine, Qatar, United Arab Emirates, Israel, Saudi Arabia, Oman, and Lebanon. The region "faces exceptional water-related challenges for the foreseeable future." Even the United States, China, and India, the world's largest water consumers, are expected to suffer "high water stress" by then.[31]

Certainly, technological developments will likely help those without potable water get more water and will help save water in agriculture, industry, and personal consumption. Some exciting technological water-saving solutions will be discussed more fully in chapter 8, "A New Water Ethic: Because Water Is Life." These possibilities hold promise, but a deeper change lies in the ethical perspectives that motivate people.

---

29. Quoted in Pearce, *When the Rivers Run Dry*, 197–98; for an intriguing discussion of water in the American West, see Marc Reisner, *Cadillac Desert: The American West and Its Disappearing Water* (New York: Viking, 1986).

30. "Climbing the World's Biggest Tree," *Economist*, December 24, 2016, 102.

31. Andrew Maddocks, Robert Samuel Young, and Paul Reig, "Ranking the World's Most Water-Stressed Countries in 2040," World Resources Institute, August 26, 2015, *www.wri.org/blog/2015/08/ranking-world%E2%80%99s-most-water-stressed-countri;es-2040*.

An Ethic of Scarcity

A Chinese student from Malaysia, studying at Seattle University, recently recounted his family's water use for bathing. Family members were given one bucket of water per week in which to wash, bathe, and rinse. Imagine his delight when he took his first shower in the university residence hall. He turned a knob and out came endless warm water. He delighted in this new abundance, until he remembered his family's use of water. Chastened by the family's scarce use, he recruited another student to help with a water project. They attached five-minute timers to the walls in the men's showers of the residence hall. It then became a "macho" manifesto to beat a five-minute timer. Scarcity was in vogue.[32]

Ethical Responses

What will motivate people and political leaders to develop the necessary programs to conserve and ensure clean water? Technological solutions are important and necessary but never sufficient. A full solution requires a profound grounding in an ethical framework. A move toward a new ethic around water, one based in particular on the principles of Catholic social teaching (CST), could help provide a strong framework for greater awareness and motivation to act.

New Water Ethic

Many have called for a new water ethic to solve the challenge of global water scarcity. Sandra Postel, founder and director of the Global Water Policy Project, notes, "We need a water ethic. . . . The essence of such an ethic is to make the protection of freshwater ecosystems a central goal in all that we do."[33] Such an ethic employs many of the CST principles outlined previously, namely, active

---

32. Personal story told to the author and a small number of students.

33. Sandra Postel, "The Missing Piece: A Water Ethic," in Brown and Schmidt, 222.

citizen participation, recognition of human dignity, and subsidiarity in communities large or small.

Cynthia Barnett called for a "Blue Revolution" in which "the fundamental belief in water as a national treasure to be preserved has to catch on at every level of society." Although people are taking greater responsibility for Earth through recycling, reusing, and so on, she argues they have done just the opposite with water—consuming more meat, buying bigger homes, growing larger lawns, and using more drinking water. Barnett does not address water scarcity experienced by people who lack fresh, clean drinking water, but her sharp analysis underscores an ethic of conservation, responsible use, and simpler patterns of consumption.

Barnett's approach involves an ethic "driven more by physical and social settings than internal compass." In other words, she believes people are inspired to act when they see what others are doing, because "consciousness catches as it spreads, becoming a belief system that is just as important as rules and regulations." For example, just as littering campaigns have caught on worldwide, a "water campaign" would target extravagant water use and waste. Finally, she notes that religion plays an important role in this ethic, referencing Pope John Paul II's January 1990 address and its influence.[34] Barnett's discussion, in addition to remarks by Postel and Catholic ethicist Christiana Zenner (formerly Peppard), call for a new water ethic to guide decisions around water scarcity and use.

Catholic Social Teaching on Scarcity

Pope John Paul II

In his January 1, 1990, World Day of Peace Message, John Paul II named a manifest injustice—"that a privileged few should continue squandering available resources, while masses of people are living in conditions of misery at the very lowest level of subsistence." His words addressed the "plundering" and "the reckless exploitation of natural resources" on the part of wealthier people and nations with lavish lifestyles, "given to instant gratification

---

34. Barnett, *Blue Revolution*, 20–21, 204, 224–25.

and consumerism." In addition to changing lifestyle patterns, he believed structural forms of poverty must be addressed in the name of justice (*WDP* 1, 6, 8, 13).

In 1991, John Paul II further developed the theme of over-consumption in his encyclical, *Centesimus annus* (*On the Hundredth Anniversary of Rerum novarum*). Contrary to the principles of both the universal destination of goods, like water, and a sense of solidarity, the consumer lifestyle is "objectively improper and often damaging to human physical and spiritual health." As a result, he again called for important changes in "established lifestyles" "to limit the waste of environmental and human resources" (*CA* 19, 36, 51).

Pontifical Council for Justice and Peace

In 2003, at the Third World Water Forum in Kyoto, the PCJP focused on the link between water and poverty in water scarcity, when "water supplies are neither sufficient nor safe." For people "living in poverty, [water scarcity] is rapidly becoming an issue crucial for life. . . . Hence linkages between water policy and ethics increasingly emerge throughout the world."[35] At the Fourth Forum in Mexico City in 2006, the council declared that wasting water is unacceptable.[36] In its 2006 "Letter to the World Water Forum" the PCJP stated forcibly that "the primary objective of all efforts [surrounding water] must be the well-being of those people who live in the poorest parts of the world and suffer most from any scarcity or misuse of water resources."[37]

The *Compendium of the Social Doctrine of the Church*[38] is an authoritative text published by the PCJP. On the topic of water, the

---

35. Quoted in Editorial, "Global Water Crisis: A Test of Solidarity," *National Catholic Reporter*, May 30, 2003, 32; the full text of the council's statement is available at *www.vatican.va*.

36. Quoted in "In Brief," *Tablet*, March 25, 2006, 41.

37. Pontifical Council for Justice and Peace, "Water: An Essential Element for Life," Mexico City, March 2006, *www.pcgp.it/dati/2012-03/09-999999/2012acquainglese .pdf; www.justpax.it/pls/pcgp/rn_pcgp_new.r_select_abstract?dicastero=2&tema=4&argo mento=0&sottoargomento=0&classe=1&id=3421&lingua=2&rif=&rif1=.*

38. Pontifical Council for Justice and Peace, *Compendium of the Social Doctrine of the Church* (Washington, DC: US Conference of Catholic Bishops, 2004).

compendium is quite strong in viewing water as a public good, particularly in relation to the poor people of the world:

> Satisfying the needs of all, especially of those who live in poverty, must guide the use of water and the services connected with it. By its very nature water cannot be treated as just another commodity among many, and it must be used in solidarity with others. The distribution of water is traditionally among the responsibilities that fall to public agencies, since water is considered a public good. (*Compendium* 484–85)

Pope Benedict XVI

Benedict XVI lays out the dire consequences of water scarcity in his 2009 encyclical, *Caritas in veritate*. He notes the great appeal that people experiencing scarcity are making to "the peoples blessed with abundance" (*CV* 17). This is a matter of "shared responsibility" in light of increasing inequalities (*CV* 22, 27). Missing "is a network of economic institutions capable of guaranteeing regular access to sufficient food and water." Stressing the principle of subsidiarity, Benedict emphasizes, "The right to food, like the right to water, has an important place within the pursuit of other rights, beginning with the fundamental right to life." Access to food and water are universal rights "without distinction" (*CV* 28).

He cites lack of food and drinkable water in underdeveloped nations as failures in understanding the duties those with more have toward those with less (*CV* 43).

The Church's moral responsibility toward creation means publically asserting that responsibility. Doing so protects "earth, water and air as gifts of creation that belong to everyone." Benedict XVI lays the groundwork for the link between human ecology and environmental ecology, noting when "human ecology is respected within society, environmental ecology also benefits" (*CV* 41, 51). Finally, Benedict XVI cautions, the "hoarding of resources, especially water, can generate serious conflicts among the peoples involved" (*CV* 51). The principles of solidarity and the universal destination of goods, such as water, apply here.

Pope Francis

In his 2015 encyclical, *Laudato si': On Care for Our Common Home*, Francis expresses great concern about water scarcity and reiterates the foundational principle that water is indispensable not only for human well-being but also "for supporting terrestrial and aquatic ecosystems"—a reminder that the debates about water involve the entire planet (*LS* 28).

African regions, in particular, concern Francis in light of water poverty: "large sectors of the population have no access to safe drinking water or experience droughts which impede agricultural production. Some countries have areas rich in water while others endure drastic scarcity" (*LS* 28). Unsafe water leads to deaths and serious water-related illnesses (*LS* 29). Some studies warn that severe water shortages are possible within a few decades and that billions of people could be affected by the consequences (*LS* 31). "The control of water by large multinational businesses" could also become a contentious issue (*LS* 31). The pope also notes that "greater scarcity of water will lead to an increase in the cost of food and the various products which depend on its use" (*LS* 31).

Francis does not propose solutions to these great injustices of scarcity and suffering. Rather, after articulating the principles of solidarity, the preferential option for the poor, equality in dignity, and the universal destination of goods, Francis speaks of the inequalities surrounding water abundance and water scarcity, "The problem of water is partly an educational and cultural issue, since there is little awareness of the seriousness of such behavior [water waste] within a context of great inequality" (*LS* 30).[39]

Finally, Francis calls for new models of global growth—new political goals serving Earth and its people—and then outlines a spirituality of humility and a new lifestyle in which people consume less and waste fewer basic resources such as water *(LS* 200ff). Far from being a less full life, "such sobriety, when lived freely and consciously, is liberating. On the contrary, it is a way of living life to the full" (*LS* 223). It is a plan to counter what Francis sees as the confusions around a consumerist culture.

---

39. Water inequality is only one example of the global inequalities that Francis addresses later in the encyclical. See *LS* 48–52.

His final words summarize his vision:

Christian spirituality proposes an alternative understanding of the quality of life, and encourages a contemplative lifestyle, capable of deep enjoyment free of the obsession with consumption. A constant flood of new consumer goods can baffle the heart and prevent us from cherishing each thing and each moment. Christian spirituality proposes a growth marked by moderation and the capacity to be happy with little. (*LS* 222)

Vatican Conference

In February 2017, following the impetus of Francis's encyclical, the Pontifical Academy of Sciences sponsored a meeting of leading policy experts, government officials, religious leaders, scholars, and development and social justice advocates to examine ways of guaranteeing that water is safe and more accessible around the globe. The delegates looked at water management and accessibility in light of such CST principles as solidarity, just distribution, preferential option for the poor, and respect for the environment. The meeting concluded with the signing of an agreement called the "Rome Declaration."[40]

Conclusion

This chapter began with a look at two families facing the realities of California's long drought, a situation of abundant water and water scarcity. The affluent Resnicks and their company fared well in terms of water access. Meanwhile, the less affluent Tijerinas did not have enough water to irrigate their wheat crop, a crop requiring less water and being more essential to the diets of ordinary people than the Resnicks' pomegranate, almond, and pistachio crops.

Next, this chapter reviewed global situations of water scarcity brought about not by a lack of water but by a scarcity of drinkable water. This water scarcity is precipitated through climate change,

40. Carol Glatz, "Vatican Invites Experts to Promote Safe, Accessible Water for Everyone," *Crux*, Catholic News Service, February 24, 2017, *https://cruxnow.com:vatican:2017:02:24:vatican-invites-experts-promote-safe-accessible-water-everyone:*.

pollution, poor agricultural practices, and increased demand for food. Scarcity fosters increasing stresses and tensions in its wake. Such stresses could, and do in some cases, lead to water wars, mainly wars fought in courts, but still significant.

Finally, this chapter explored the ethical framework needed to guide changes in policy and lifestyle related to water access and scarcity. CST sees global water scarcity through the lens of major principles, such as the universal destination of Earth's goods; the common good of all peoples, particularly of poor and marginalized people; and equal access to freshwater, as essential to life. These latter reflections raise important questions around the basic right to water. Do people have a fundamental right to clean, drinkable water? Is water a public matter? Or can it be privatized and seen as a commodity? These are important questions for later discussions.

Review Questions

1. Why do the Resnicks have such an abundance of water?
2. Why is water scarcity increasing? What are the main factors?
3. What is the largest crop in the United States?
4. How is water wasted in agriculture, industry, and personal use?
5. How does a growing population impact water scarcity?
6. What is Barnett's approach to a water ethic? Is it practical?
7. What does Christian spirituality add to the argument for addressing water scarcity, according to Francis?
8. How does the preferential option for the poor relate to water scarcity?

Discussion Questions

1. How might the Resnicks and the Tijerinas save water?
2. What suggestions would you make to leaders in your area to alleviate situations of water scarcity and waste?
3. What measures can a university or college take to cut back on water use?

4. Which approach in the CST documents is most helpful in persuading the public to use less water? Why?

5. Which principles of CST did you find most compelling in considering water scarcity? Why?

CHAPTER

Extraction from the Earth
Impacts of Mining and Fracking on Water and People

In the summer of 2016, the Standing Rock Sioux and their supporters were in a standoff with the North Dakota Morton County Sheriff's Department and the National Guard. At issue was construction of a final section of the Dakota Access Pipeline (DAPL), the longest crude-oil pipeline in the continental United States. Completion meant digging under the Missouri River, coming close to Lake Oahe, the Standing Rock Sioux's water supply, which they view as sacred. In July, a small number of the Standing Rock people protested the completion, grabbing the nation's attention and inspiring members of more than two hundred Native American tribes and supporters, including war veterans, to "stand" with the Sioux for freshwater and tribal sovereignty.[1]

Earlier, in spring 2015, young people at the encampment realized that their elders had little support for the struggle. Moved to act, one young mother, Bobbi Joan Three Legs, a long-distance runner from Standing Rock, proposed a 500-mile relay run from the camp to the US Army Corps of Engineers headquarters in Omaha to deliver a letter asking the corps to deny a permit request that would allow the Dakota Access Pipeline to cross the Missouri River.

---

1. Wes Enzinna, "Crude Awakening," *Mother Jones*, January-February 2017, 34–37; and Louise Erdrich, "Holy Rage: Lessons from Standing Rock," *New Yorker*, December 22, 2016, *www.newyorker.com/news/news-desk/holy=-rage-lessons-from-standing-rock?mbid-nl.161222.*

Private companies pursuing projects involving public land and waters must acquire a permit from the Army corps in order to undertake such projects.

An Army Corps representative agreed to meet with tribal members, and the young people were urged to call off the run. However, the youth believed the run would unite young people from Sioux reservations (the seven bands of the Sioux organized as the Seven Council Fires). The run was also a rich cultural symbol: before Europeans brought horses, long-distance runners had made the connections among the scattered tribes. On April 24, 2015, the runners set off.

On May 3, a corps representative met with them; however, the young people wanted to continue. So on July 9, they announced via YouTube.com that they would organize a 2,000-mile run to Washington, D.C., and deliver a petition to the national corps headquarters. However, on July 26, they learned that the corps had approved the pipeline easements. The focus now shifted back to the camp, even as the runners decided to continue on to Washington.

Activists at the camp used Facebook to urge others to rise to the high standard set by the youth. Soon hundreds of people began to pour into the camp from across North America.[2] As a symbol of the young people's work, members of the Indigenous Youth Council brought water to the police standing on the other side of the barriers; two officers refused, but one accepted, spilling the water on his shirt over his heart. That officer and one of the youths then bowed heads and prayer together.[3]

Despite an Obama administration request to postpone construction, CEO of Energy Transfer Partners, Kelcy Warren, announced on Election Day 2016 that tunneling under Lake Oahe would begin in two weeks. Further violence was prevented when the Army corps decided the pipeline would remain uncompleted pending further review of its environmental impact. Chanse Adams-Zavalla, a protestor from California, said, "Even if somehow, someway, they build

2. Saul Elbein, "The Seventh Generation," *New York Times Magazine*, February 5, 2017, 24–25, 28–31, 49.

3. Erdrich, "Holy Rage."

this pipeline, they've inadvertently sparked a whole generation of us to fight for Mother Earth."[4]

The victory for water was short-lived, however; the Trump administration quickly allowed the pipeline to be completed.[5] By March 28, 2017, Energy Transfer Partners announced that oil would flow through the DAPL, and on June 1, the first flow commenced. However, the Standing Rock Sioux sued in federal court to stop the flow, and to the amazement of many, a federal judge ruled that any permits already granted must be reconsidered in order to complete the DAPL.[6]

Hopi and Navajo Peoples and Water

Another violent extraction process played out in the southwestern United States, again involving indigenous peoples—the Hopi and Navajo tribes—around mining.

In 1964, Peabody Western Coal entered into an agreement with Navajo people and two years later with the Hopi peoples of northern Arizona. The tribes would cede mineral and water rights of the Black Mesa aquifer, the tribes' main source of drinking water and water for livestock and farming, to Peabody in exchange for badly needed funds for development of the tribes. Peabody Energy developed two coal strip mines on the Black Mesa reservation: the Black Mesa Mine and the Kayenta Mine. What the Hopi and Navajo did not know at the time was that John Boyden, the attorney who negotiated the agreement on behalf of the tribes, was actually on Peabody's payroll. Boyden said the company would only take "a cup" of the huge "underwater sea" (Black Mesa aquifer).

The severe decline in potable water and in the number of fresh springs that the Hopi subsequently suffered was, the tribe alleged,

---

4. Enzinna, "Crude Awakening," 34–37; Erdrich, "Holy Rage."

5. Note: on February 5, 2017, US President Donald Trump issued an executive order to complete construction of the pipeline; Trump also has a financial interest in Energy Transfer Partners.

6. Lynda V. Mapes, "Federal Judge Rejects Dakota Access Pipeline Permits, Calls for Do-over," *Seattle Times*, June 15, 2017, *www.seattletimes.com/seattle-news /environment/federal-judge-rejects-dakota-access-pipeline-permits-calls-for-do-over/*.

due to Peabody's mining. Vernon Masayesva, Hopi tribal chairperson from 1990 to 1994, reflected on the huge mistake the tribe made in the 1964 deal: "We sold our soul to this company."[7]

The extraction processes used to send Black Mesa coal to a power plant took more than three million gallons of pristine water from the aquifer daily, much more than "a cup." By 2005, the Black Mesa mine was using four thousand acre-feet of water (325,851,429 gallons) per year, in an area that receives only twelve inches of rain per year. Kenyata Mine coal was sent to the Navajo Generating Station coal plant, held in a silo, and shipped.[8] The Kayenta mine sucked up about 1,200 acre-feet (almost 392 million gallons) of groundwater per year from the aquifer, while the Navajo Generating Station pulled up some 28,000 acre-feet (9 billion gallons) per year from Lake Powell. Peabody was extracting far more water from the aquifer than could be recharged by nature: springs and streams dried up; potable water declined.[9]

Because the Hopi and Navajo nations had signed a contract with Peabody, there was not much legally they could do. In 2002 the Navajo and Hopi tribal councils passed resolutions asking Peabody not to use Navajo aquifer waters to transport the coal to the processing plant (a small step, but an example of the tribes beginning to exercise their water rights). Meanwhile, over the years residents in the area, local grassroots organizations, and national environmental groups called for an end to Peabody's mining practices. These were moral arguments; no legal challenge could be made. The impact of this story is important in part because it underlies the tragedy in which many indigenous peoples find themselves: cheated or sometimes coaxed into selling or lending certain rights to land and water to private corporations in exchange for the companies' promise of pay.

The plant associated with the mines is scheduled to close in 2019, twenty-five years ahead of schedule. Hopi and Navajo water,

---

7. "Hopi Land," from *In the Light of Reverence*, DVD, produced and directed by Christopher McLeod (Berkeley, CA: Sacred Land Film Project, 2002). For a full account of the controversy, refer to "The Black Mesa Controversy," *Cultural Survival Quarterly*, December 2005, *www.culturalsurvival.org/publications/cultural-survival-quarterly/black -mesa-controversy.*

8. Enei Begaye, "The Black Mesa Controversy," *Cultural Survival Quarterly*, December 2005, *www.culturalsurvival.org/publications/cultural-survival-quarterly /black-mesa-controversy.*

9. "Hopi Land," from *In the Light of Reverence*, and "The Black Mesa Controversy."

air, and land will become cleaner. However, the two mines forced people to relocate, ruined grazing lands, dried up sacred springs, and destroyed ancestral sacred sites. In addition, the tribes' much-needed revenue and almost one thousand mining jobs will be lost. Nevertheless, Masayesva, now executive director of the Black Mesa Trust, said, "I am very happy that Black Mesa Trust's struggle to save sacred waters on Black Mesa will finally end. It is time to begin healing the ecological-cultural landscape."[10]

Problems Ahead: Water in Trouble

These stories underscore larger, systemic policies and issues around extractive enterprises such as mining and fracking, as well as the impact these technologies have on indigenous peoples. It is important to explore the technologies in more detail.

Mining

Mining is usually related to gold, silver, precious metals, uranium, and coal, using and contaminating large amounts of water. Sulfide mining involves extracting metals such as gold and copper from a sulfide-rich ore area. When the sulfides are exposed to air and water, sulfuric acid is created, "acid mine drainage" (AMD); the mix threatens to poison the nearby water, environment, and communities. The acid mine drainage "poisons water forever; once AMD pollution begins, it is very difficult to contain or remediate the problem."[11] In the United States, acid mine drainage, mostly from abandoned mines, "pollutes an estimated 12,000 miles of streams throughout the West."[12]

Around the globe, mining waste, that is, large amounts of water, chemicals, and elements released in the mining process, make their way back into waterways as pollution. In Brazil, for example, the

---

10. Quoted in Jonathan Thompson, "The West's Coal Giant Is Going Down," *High Country News*, March 30, 2017, 5–6.

11. Mining Action Group, "What Is Sulfide Mining?," 2016, Upper Peninsula Mining Coalition, *http://savethewildup.org/about/sulfide-mining-101/*.

12. Laura Pritchett, "Hardrock Revision," *High Country News*, November 28, 2011, 20.

gold-mining industry deposits more than 130 tons of mercury into the Tapajoz River.[13] Many other examples reveal the same story: mining uses large amounts of water during extraction and refining and then produces unusable, contaminated wastewater—clean water in, wastewater out.

Because the "out" water is so highly contaminated, it is usually not released into waterways in developed countries. Instead, such toxic brews and pollutants are held in aboveground disposal ponds. One of the best-known such ponds in the United States is the Berkeley Pit, near Butte, Montana, a site filled with acidic, toxic wastewater that today forms an open, contaminated lake.[14] On November 28, 2016, a large flock of some ten thousand snow geese landed in the pit's lake in an attempt to avoid a snowstorm. Thousands died due to the lake's poisonous water.[15]

Coal, the King Deposed

For decades, energy production in America relied mostly on coal, until the development of oil, gas, and hydro-energy plants in the early 1900s and nuclear power plants in the 1950s.[16] In 2016, coal still supplied 33 percent of the nation's energy, a sharp drop from the high of 55 percent in 1955.[17] The decline in the use of coal owing to cheaper natural gas has led several global companies, such as Peabody Western Coal, to file for bankruptcy.[18]

---

13. Philip Ball, *Life's Matrix,: A Biography of Water* (New York: Farrar, Straus and Giroux, 1999), 353–54; Marq de Villiers, *Water: The Fate of Our Most Precious Resource* (New York: Houghton-Mifflin, 2000), 89. For further discussion, see Gary L. Chamberlain, *Troubled Waters: Religion, Ethics, and the Global Water Crisis* (Lanham, MD: Rowman and Littlefield, 2008), 79–114.

14. "Berkeley Pit History," *PitWatch: Berkeley Pit News and Info, www.pitwatch.org /berkeley-pit-history/5/.*

15. "Snow Geese Update," *PitWatch: Berkeley Pit News and Info,* December 9, 2016, *www.pitwatch.org/snow-geese-update/.*

16. Cf. ProCon.org for a succinct history of energy sources, June 13, 2013, *http:// alternativeenergy.procon.org/view.timeline.php?timelineID=000015.*

17. "Today in Energy," US Energy Information Administration (EIA), December 8, 2016, *www.eia.gov/todayinenergy/archive.php?my=Sep2016.*

18. Arathy Nair, "Peabody Chapter 11 Tops String of U.S. Coal Bankruptcies," *Reuters,* April 15, 2016, *www.reuters.com/article/us-usa-coal-bankruptcy-idUSKCN0XC2KQ.*

When considering human health, water, and environmental concerns, coal mining has always been a "dirty" business. "King Coal"[19] used and abused water. Since the 1960s, a cheaper and more efficient technology has moved into America's Appalachian coal country. "Mountaintop removal" is a process in which the tops of mountains are blasted away with explosives to reveal coal veins. The resulting debris is dumped into nearby ravines and hollows, blocking and polluting freshwater streams. The EPA estimates that more than two thousand miles of headwater streams have been buried or poisoned.[20]

Aquifer Depletion

An even more immediate threat involves aquifer depletion—that is, excessive use of water from aquifers, or underground, natural lakes. One of the most important aquifers in the United States, the Ogallala, stretches from Nebraska through the Midwest to Colorado, New Mexico, and Texas. From about 1950, when substantial irrigation in the aquifer region began, to 2013, the aquifer experienced a decline of 15.4 feet; the period from 2011 to 2013 alone saw a decline of 2.1 feet in the aquifer. In acre-feet, that meant a decline of 266.7 million acre-feet (almost 87 million gallons) since about 1950, and a 36 million acre-feet (11.75 million gallon) decline between 2011 and 2013.[21]

A 2015 study revealed that twenty-one out of the thirty-seven largest aquifers worldwide "are being drained faster than they can refill." The damage is not only to drinking water and agriculture, but

---

19. *King Coal* was the term the US Catholic Bishops of Appalachia used to describe the role of coal in the lives of the people of Appalachia. With support from powerful interests and politicians, coal "reigned" supreme in the economic and political life of the area. See Catholic Committee of Appalachia, *This Land Is Home to Me* (Prestonsburg, KY: Catholic Committee of Appalachia, 1975).

20. "Ecological Impacts of Mountaintop Removal," *Appalachian Voices*, http://appvoices.org/end-mountaintop-removal/ecology/.

21. Virginia McGuire, "Water-Level Changes and Change in Water in Storage in the High Plains Aquifer, Predevelopment to 2013 and 2011 to 2013," US Geological Survey, Reston, Virginia: 2014, *https://pubs.usgs.gov/sir/2014/5218/pdf/sir2014_5218.pdf*.

also aquifer mining also "damages wetlands, makes land sink, and contributes to sea-level rise."[22]

Hydraulic Fracturing, or Fracking

Since the early 1990s, hydraulic fracturing, or fracking, has formed a new approach to natural gas and oil production. It involves first drilling vertically deep into the earth and then drilling horizontally from the well bottom and using large amounts of water, under high pressure, to force oil and gas from shale.[23] An industry article explains the processes used after initial drilling and extraction have drawn out the easily accessed sources. "By injecting liquids and gases, producers are able to force residual oil and gas deposits to the surface to be extracted." In 2015, such drilling ranked as the second largest use of water globally.[24]

On the pro side, as a "bridge fuel" between use of coal and use of renewable energy sources, such as sun and wind, natural gas is relatively clean. It is also cheap compared with other fossil fuels. On the con side, fracking for natural gas releases methane, a powerful greenhouse gas, that accelerates climate change.[25]

Fracking: Water Contamination

By 2011, a Duke University study involving sixty-eight water wells in northeastern Pennsylvania and southern New York had found a strong link between fracking and drinking water contamination "so severe that some faucets can be lit on fire."[26] Yet the EPA concluded, in 2015, that there was no evidence fracking contaminated drinking water.

22. "Water Mining. Groundwater Depletion," December 22, 2016, *www.google.com/search?source=hp&ei=ck0CWqqOM4uMjwPG2qLAAg&q=aquifer+depletion+worldwide&oq=aquifer+depletion+worldwide&gs_l=psy ab.3..0i22i30k1.1668.12237.0.14616.29.28.1.0.0.0.143.2333.21j.*

23. Bruce Lieberman, "Pros and Cons: Promise, Pitfalls of Natural Gas," *Yale Climate Connections*, July 7, 2016, *www.yaleclimateconnections.org/2016/07/pros-and-cons-the-promise-and-pitfalls-of-natural-gas.*

24. Xylem Let's Solve Water, "Water Use in Oil and Gas," 2015, *www.wwdmag.com/sites/wwdmag.com/files/XB037_Xylem_Water_Use_in_Oil&Gas_Brochure_sm.pdf.*

25. Lieberman, "Pros and Cons."

26. Abrahm Lustgarten, "Scientific Study Links Flammable Drinking Water to Fracking," *ProPublica*, May 9, 2011, *www.propublica.org/article/scientific-study-links-flammable-drinking-water-to-fracking.*

Hydrologic fracturing, or "fracking," can lead to toxic water, and in some cases, the water actually can ignite into flames.

A March 2016 study from Stanford University provided "the first-ever unequivocal link between fracking and groundwater contamination."[27] In December 2016, the EPA reversed its stance in an updated study of the connection between fracking and groundwater contamination, concluding, "The oil-and-gas extraction technique can taint the water supply in certain circumstances. Contamination has occurred following surface spills of fracking fluid."[28]

Fracking: Wastewater

There remains the question of what to do with fracking wastewater, which accompanies the gas and oil brought to the surface. At present, 10–40 percent of the fluid injected underground returns to the surface as wastewater. This wastewater, called "produced water," is contaminated and cannot be reused for agricultural, industrial, or consumer purposes. The amount of water brought up translates to

27. Elizabeth Shogren, "Followup," *High Country News*, May 2, 2016, 5; "Fire Water," *Economist*, June 25, 2013; and "Frack Check WV," *www.frackcheckwv.net /impacts/water/*.

28. "EPA Backtracks on Fracking Safety," *The Week*, December 23–30, 2016, 6; see also "Ticker," *Time*, December 26, 2016–January 2, 2017, 16.

about three million gallons per frack job. This water must be trucked away, at great expense, and disposed of in a deep-well injection site.

Fracking: Other Impacts

Besides the impacts mentioned, many experts link fracking with increased seismic activity. On November 6, 2016, a 5.0 magnitude earthquake shook land around Cushing, Oklahoma, a major fracking area.[29] Oklahoma used to average three quakes per year. Paralleling the state's increase in hydraulic fracturing, this number rose dramatically: 109 quakes in 2013, climbing to 623 quakes in 2016.[30] In April 2015, the *New Yorker* reported that nearly two dozen professional papers found that fracking and earthquakes are likely linked.[31] Despite these concerns, the US government has not banned fracking.

Fracking Bans

However, controversies around fracking have led several states to ban fracking, such as New York, Vermont, and Maryland.[32] Between 2011 and 2015, France, Bulgaria, Scotland, and Germany banned fracking. In addition, the United Kingdom, Romania, Denmark, Ireland, South Africa, and the Czech Republic passed moratoriums.[33] Other efforts nationally and internationally continue.[34]

---

29. John Hockenberry, "Oil Town Hit by Earthquakes Isn't Ready to Turn off the Pipelines Just Yet," *The Takeaway*, National Public Radio, January 24, 2017; Jeanna Bryner, "5.0-Magnitude Earthquake Hits Oklahoma," *LiveScience*, November 6, 2016, *www.livescience.com/56767-earthquake-shakes-oklahoma.html*.

30. "Earthquakes in Oklahoma," *https://earthquakes.ok.gov*.

31. "Exploring the Link Between Earthquakes and Oil and Gas Disposal Wells," *https://stateimpact.npr.org/oklahoma/tag/earthquakes/*.

32. Food and Water Watch, *2016 Progress against Fracking in the US*, brochure, April 2016. See also Devin Henry, "Maryland governor signs fracking ban into law." *The Hill*, April 4, 2017, *http://thehill.com/policy/energy-environment/327266-maryland-governor-signs-fracking-ban-into-law*.

33. Kate Good, "These 4 Countries Have Banned Fracking—Why Can't the US Get On Board?," *One Green Planet*, February 11, 2015, *www.onegreenplanet.org/environment/countries-except-united-states-that-have-banned-fracking/*.

34. Cf. Food and Water Watch, "Keep the Tap Water Safe," *https://keeptapwatersafe.org/global-bans-on-fracking/* for updates on bans and moratoriums.

Catholics Respond to Extractive Industries

Many Catholic organizations, lay leaders, religious communities, and bishops in the United States and around the world have addressed the problems and concerns they have with extractive industries, such as mining and fracking, in relation to the harm to people, particularly to indigenous communities, and to the environment. A few examples follow.

The United States: Coal and Fossil Fuels

In 1975 the bishops of the Appalachia region published a powerful, prophetic, and poetic letter, "This Land is Home to Me." They were addressing the poverty and powerlessness of the people of the Appalachian region, which extends from southern New York to northern Alabama, Mississippi, and Georgia. In looking at large coal companies and their political and economic power, the bishops note that the renewal of coal in the 1970s and beyond, "would probably not make its people any more powerful. Instead, they would live a different kind of powerlessness, the powerlessness of isolated little people in the face of the most powerful corporate giants on this earth." Not mincing their words, the bishops call the dominance of King Coal "The Worship of an Idol" and note, "The way of life which these corporate giants create is called by some 'technological rationalization.' . . . Too often, however, its forces become perverted, hostile to the dignity of the earth and of its people. Its destructive growth patterns pollute the air, foul the water, and rape the land." The poverty of the people and the waste of the land and water result from the practices of "The kings . . . who control big coal, and the profit and power which come with it."[35]

The document brought new energy to church workers in the area, in particular communities of women religious who arrived in large numbers along with groups organized from around the country. The Catholic Committee of Appalachia organized courses on social justice.[36] However, some forty years later, in 2015, those same women

---

35. Catholic Committee of Appalachia, "This Land Is Home to Me."

36. David Andrews, "Faith Community Should Lead," *National Catholic Reporter*, August 28, 2013, *www.ncronline.org/blogs/eco-catholic/global-fight-against-fracking-faith-community-should-lead*.

religious communities see, sadly, that poverty, powerlessness, fouling of water, and destruction of the land continue.[37]

The United States: Fracking

Catholic conferences in New York and Ohio, as well as some bishops, have posed several key ethical questions around fracking to government officials based on CST.[38] The USCCB Environmental Justice Program and the Catholic Campaign for Human Development have worked together on water issues, and in their 2014 brief statement, the bishops challenge extractive enterprises, such as coal mining and fracking, that contaminate water with chemicals and so threaten people's health. The bishops note that although community groups have been struggling to keep watersheds clean, "the fracking industry has raised new concerns."[39] In spring 2013, the ninety-year-old National Catholic Rural Life Conference reviewed the dangers of fracking and pushed for an ethical analysis based on CST in the fracking debate in relation to water, agriculture, and labor.[40]

The United States: Mountaintop Removal

The US bishops have also weighed in on the controversial practice of mountaintop removal described previously in this chapter. In a 1998 resolution, the bishops outlined the practice's harmful impacts: "severe and unlawful damage to the homes of persons, and the millions and millions of tons of earth and rock dumped into the valleys

37. Dan Stockman, "Appalachian Coal Country, Where Sisters See Little Change in 40 Years," *National Catholic Reporter*, March 2, 2017. *www.ncronline.org/preview /appalachian-coal-country-where-sisters-see-little-change-40-years*.

38. Dennis Sadowski, "Catholic Voices Raise Moral Concerns in Country's Fracking Debates," *Catholic News Service*, December 11, 2013, *www.catholicnews.com /services/englishnews/2013/catholic-voices-raise-moral-concerns-in-country-s-fracking -debates.cfm*.

39. "Working on the Margins," USCCB Environmental Justice Program & Catholic Campaign for Human Development, 2014, *www.usccb.org/issues-and-action /.../cchd-ejp-funded-groups-chart-2014.pdf*.

40. David Andrews, "Faith Community Should Lead."

next to these mountains totally destroying the springs and the head waters of streams." The Catholic Committee of Appalachia members, led by the bishops, resolve that they will implore elected officials to stop the practice.[41] Though the practice continues, Catholic activists have multiplied efforts to stop it, arguing that Catholics "can insist that their electric utilities refuse to source coal from mountaintop removal mines and, better yet, provide renewable-power alternatives to coal." Also, Catholics can reduce their own consumption of products that make coal mining and resulting water damage necessary.[42]

Worldwide: Fossil Fuels

On the feast of St. Francis, September 3, 2016, several Catholic institutions and other faith communities announced that they will divest from fossil fuels; many leaders cite the impact of Pope Francis's 2015 encyclical *Laudato si': On Care for Our Common Home* as an inspiration to take action. Among others, the organizations include the Jesuits in English Canada, Presentation Society of Australia and Papua New Guinea, Missionary Society of St. Columban, Salesian Sisters of Don Bosco-Daughters of Mary Help in Milan and Naples, and Sisters of St. Mary (SSM) Health, serving the midwestern United States.[43]

Worldwide: Fracking

A recent report by the Sisters of Mercy noted that Catholic groups around the world have expressed great concerns about fracking. Mercy sisters have been outspoken against fracking in Argentina, Australia, England, Ireland, Canada, New Zealand, and the United States. Together they formed the Mercy International Association's

41. Catholic Committee of Appalachia, "Resolution on Mountain Top Removal," 1998. *http://ccappal.org/publications/statements-resolutions/resolution-on-mountaintop-removal.*

42. Kyle Kramer, "Though the Mountains May Fall: The Cost of Mountain Top Removal," *U.S. Catholic,* April 2012, 12–16, *www.uscatholic.org/culture/environment /2012/03/though-mountains-may-fall-cost-mountain-top-removal.*

43. 350.org, "Catholic Institutions around the World Announce They Are Divesting from Fossil Fuel Extraction, Marking the Largest Faith-based Divestment Announcement," October 3, 2016, *https://350.org/press-release/catholic-institutions -around-the-world-announce-they-are-divesting-from-fossil-fuel-extraction-marking-the -largest-faith-based-divestment-announcement/.* See the site for comments from leaders.

Global Action Network, an environmental and social justice advocacy group that focuses on fracking's negative impacts on the health, land, and water of indigenous peoples. Their emphasis involves issues of racism and "particular concern for women."[44]

Worldwide: Mining

Catholic leaders around the world—especially in Latin America, where mining often takes place on indigenous people's lands—have become very vocal in opposition to mining. As far back as 2005, the bishop of a diocese in Patagonia, Argentina, led criticism of cyanide use in mining, leading to a ban on a new gold-silver development that year. (The ban was overturned, however, in 2012, but no project has yet been approved in the area.) Then in 2009 another Argentinian bishop led opposition to a massive Navidad silver mine project; Navidad is owned by a multinational Canadian company, Pan American Silver Corp. Earlier in 2010 indigenous communities around the site of the Navidad mine had demanded the right to pick their own mining development model.[45]

In March 2015, the Latin American bishops at the Inter-American Commission on Human Rights petitioned the governments of the United States and Canada to hold companies operating from the two countries in South and Central America to the laws that protect indigenous communities and vulnerable groups, local economies, rivers, and the environment. Then at a key meeting in Santo Domingo, Dominican Republic, in September 2016, the Catholic Churches and Mining Network, a Catholic organization of bishops, religious, and laypeople, argued that church leaders and others must help find alternatives to "mega-mining" operations.[46]

---

44. Sisters of Mercy, "Mercy and Fracking," *www.sistersofmercy.org/files/documents/resources/Justice/Mercy-and-Fracking.pdf.*

45. Luis Manuel Claps, NACLA, "Mountains of Faith?: The Church Takes on Large-Scale Mining," December 2, 2013, *https://nacla.org/blog/2013/12/2/mountains-faith-church- takes-large-scale-mining;* and Shafique Khokhar, "For Catholic Church, Mining Threatens India's Tribal Peoples," *Asia News,* May 22, 2015, *www.asianews.it/news-en/For-Catholic-Church,-"mining-threatens-India's-tribal-peoples"-34315.html.*

46. Ezra Fieser, "Latin American Christians Blast 'Mega-mining,' *Crux,* Catholic News Service, September 9, 2016, *https://cruxnow.com/global-church/2016/09/09/christians-leaders-latin-american-say-mining-causes-damage-not-benefits/.*

Finally, a series of events in 2017 emphasized the important and powerful role of the Catholic Church in opposition to large-scale mining operations and harm to water, indigenous people, and lands. In April 2017, a Peruvian court ruled on a key case supported by Catholic Church leaders that indigenous communities do have a right to be consulted about drilling on their land, a right that can be extended to other extractive industries such as mining.[47] In Brazil, the Pan-Amazonian Ecclesial Network (REPAM), a network linked to the Latin American Conference of Catholic Bishops (CELAM), joined the outcry against the August 2017 decision of Brazil's new president, Michel Temar, to open some 17,800 square miles of the Renca reserve—called the "lungs of the world" and home to more than 3,700 indigenous peoples—to exploitation by multinational corporations. By the end of September, Temar's government had reversed itself and restored the conditions of the area.[48]

Also in August 2017, the Canadian bishops challenged Canadian mining companies by issuing a letter condemning "the unethical way Canadian mining companies have been operating in Latin America or other regions of the world."

Addressed to Canadian Prime Minister Justin Trudeau, the letter calls for the appointment of an independent legal overseer (ombudsman) to examine complaints against mining companies, especially from poor and indigenous communities. The Canadian Catholic Organization for Development and Peace has been calling for the examination of such complaints since 2013.[49]

---

47. Barbara J. Fraser, "Peruvian Court: Indigenous Communities Must Be Consulted before Drilling," *National Catholic Reporter*, Catholic News Service, April 5, 2017, *www.ncronline.org/blogs/eco-catholic/peruvian-court-indigenous-communities-must-be-consulted-drilling*.

48. For more information see Karla Mendes, "Tribal Leaders Worried as Battle to Open up the Amazon to Mining Rages," Reuters News Service, *www.reuters.com/article/us-brazil-amazon-mining/tribal-leaders-worried-as-battle-to-open-up-the-amazon-to-mining-rages-idUSKCN1BC4X3*; also "Brazil Scraps Bid to Mine Amazon Natural Reserve," September 26, 2017, *https://phys.org/news/2017-09-brazil-scraps-amazon-natural-reserve.html*.

49. "We Cannot Accept the Unethical Way Canadian Mining Companies Have Been Operating in Latin America," *Catholic World News*, August 18, 2017, *http://angelqueen.org/2017/08/18/canadian-bishops-we-cannot-accept-the-unethical-way-canadian-mining-companies-have-been-operating-in-latin-america*; also Michael Swan, "Digging for the Truth," *The Catholic Register*, September 3, 2017, *www.catholicregister.org/home/international/item/25963-digging-for-the-truth*.

Papal Leadership

Pope John Paul II, *The Ecological Crisis: A Common Responsibility*

In his 1990 World Day of Peace address, John Paul II argued that world peace is threatened "by the plundering of natural resources," such as water (*WDP* 1). He reminds readers that Earth is a "common heritage, the fruits of which are for the benefit of all," and not just for a "privileged few" who "squander available resources, while most people are living in conditions of misery" (*WDP* 7). For John Paul II, damage to the environment is a key moral issue, and the pope specifically refers to the "urgent need to find a solution to the treatment and disposal of toxic wastes," important elements of mining and fracking enterprises (*WDP* 10).

John Paul II also advocated for reconciliation between indigenous peoples and nonindigenous. His brief but historic address on November 29, 1986, at Alice Springs, Australia, to "The Aborigines and Torres Strait Islanders" outlined the contributions that aboriginal peoples had made to the vitality and well-being of the country: "You are part of Australia and Australia is part of you. And the Church herself in Australia will not be fully the Church that Jesus wants her to be until you have made your contribution to her life and until that contribution has been joyfully received by others."[50]

Pope Benedict XVI, *Caritas in veritate* (*Charity in Truth*)

Benedict XVI expresses an even greater urgency concerning the "exploitation of non-renewable resources" (*CV* 49). For the pope there is a strong theological dimension: "This responsibility is concerned with the whole of creation, which must not be bequeathed to future generations depleted of its resources" (*CV* 50). Humans are stewards of creation and part of a covenant between humans and the environment, involving "the creative love of God" (*CV* 50). He

---

50. "Address of John Paul II to the Aborigines and Torres Strait Islanders," November 29, 1986, *http://w2.vatican.va/content/john-paul-ii/en/speeches/1986/november /documents/hf_jp-ii_spe_19861129_aborigeni-alice-springs-australia.html.*

worries that "the hoarding of resources, especially water, can generate serious conflicts." The ethical criteria are not efficiency but the greater global common good and a preferential option for poor people. Benedict XVI understands that the well-being of humanity is directly tied to the well-being of Earth (*CV* 51).

Pope Francis, *Laudato si'*

While Francis was archbishop of Buenos Aires, Argentina, he signed a statement describing the large mining projects in Patagonia as "affecting the survival of indigenous communities." He then helped establish the Pastoral Team for Ministry with Indigenous Peoples, (ENDEPA), to assist indigenous peoples in struggles for land titles and clean waters and against mining projects.[51]

It is no surprise then that Francis in his encyclical on the environment considers the ethical issues involved in resource extraction generally and looks at problems connected to mining (*LS* 29, 35). Degradation of water resources, which often accompanies mining, receives special attention (*LS* 41).

Francis introduces three new tools of ethical analysis. First, he speaks of the concept of an "ecological debt . . . between the global north and south, connected to commercial imbalances and the disproportionate use of natural resources by certain countries over long periods of time," in particular, harm caused by gold and copper mining (*LS* 51).

Second, his theme of debt is a key to his assessment of the impacts of resource extraction on developing countries and especially on indigenous cultures. Francis insists that indigenous peoples must be consulted as "the principal dialogue partners" when projects affecting their lands, waters, and cultures are involved: "For them, land is a gift from God and from their ancestors, a sacred space with which they need to interact if they are to maintain their identity and values" (*LS* 146). Francis is concerned about the pressures on indigenous communities "to abandon their homelands to make room for agricultural or mining projects that are undertaken without regard for the degradation of nature and culture" (*LS* 146).

---

51. Claps, NACLA, "Mountains of Faith?"

The environmental community's third assessment tool is the "precautionary principle."[52] Francis explains: "If objective information suggests that serious and irreversible damage may result, a project should be halted or modified, even in the absence of indisputable proof. Here the burden of proof is reversed" (*LS* 186).

In other words, environmental ventures can be ethical only when "the economic and social costs of using up shared environmental resources are recognized with transparency and fully borne by those who incur them, not by other peoples or future generations" (*LS* 195). In these statements, Francis posits water as "scarce and indispensable" and asserts that humans have a "fundamental right" to water; "this indisputable fact overrides any other assessment of environmental impact" (*LS* 185).

Cultural Ecology

Finally, Francis introduces the concept of cultural ecology, intertwined with natural ecology. Respect for the rights of people and cultures involves an understanding of the historical process "which takes place within a cultural context" and requires the active involvement of local communities "from within their proper culture" (*LS* 144). Extractive enterprises can actually lead to the disappearance of a social system, of an entire culture through the imposition of a "dominant lifestyle linked to a single form of production" (*LS* 145). Francis, like John Paul II and Benedict XVI, argues that it is time to set limits on growth in developed countries, so other peoples can be provided resources for healthy growth (*LS* 193).

General Principles and Conclusion

As questions arise over extractive practices that impact indigenous lands and people—the pollution of scarce water and water use in fracking and mining—basic principles become even more important. The common good now extends to the good of the entire planet. CST dramatically exposes and criticizes environmental and cultural

---

52. The precautionary principle involves "the precept that an action should not be taken if the consequences are uncertain and potentially dangerous," *www.dictionary.com/browse/precautionary-principle*.

racism against indigenous people. The importance of participation, equality, and dignity is underscored. The principle of the universal destination of created goods, such as water, dictates that those resources be developed and used for all.

Review Questions

1. What are the main difficulties involved in extraction mining?
2. In what ways is aquifer depletion mining?
3. What is fracking?
4. What are the main advantages and disadvantages of fracking?
5. What is the link, if any, between fracking and earthquakes? Between fracking and water pollution?
6. What new dimensions to CST were added by John Paul II? By Benedict XVI? By Francis?

Discussion Questions

1. Is mining still necessary? What regulations should there be to govern mining?
2. If a natural gas company using fracking wanted to drill a well in your town or city, what regulations, if any, would you use to ensure that area water remained safe?
3. What arguments from Catholic social teaching support or criticize extraction enterprises?
4. How does Pope Francis's position on "cultural integrity" support the arguments of the Standing Rock Sioux of North Dakota or the Hopi of Arizona?

Selling Water
Privatization of a Scarce Resource

Two stories introduce the issues surrounding the sale of water, a common good belonging to all: private bottled water and privatization of water delivery systems.

Trip to Belize

"You can't do this!" exclaimed Trena. A group of Seattle University students and I were leaving a hostel in Belize City, Belize, ready to return to Seattle after a ten-day service trip. Trena was a Jesuit Volunteer International American working in Belize City who had spent nearly two years among the Belize people witnessing poverty and seeing the ways in which developed nations' consumptive practices were impacting Belizean peoples. She pointed to a huge box stuffed with empty plastic water bottles. During their time in the city, the students had bought and drunk bottled water and, rooted in first-world expectations, assumed someone would recycle the plastic bottles.

Students had been told that water in Belize City was safe to drink. But they were used to buying bottled water on campus and thought it more hygienic. Trena patiently explained that most Belizeans could not afford bottled water (which had just been introduced to the country that year), that it had been imported by companies trying to make a profit, and that Belize had no way to recycle or reuse the plastic bottles. The bottles ended up as trash, a problem for an already overloaded dump system. This sparked an intense discussion on the way home and later at the university about poverty, private bottled water, and the problems of clean water.

Water Wars Begin: Bolivia

In 1999, citizens of Cochabamba, Bolivia, began a long struggle for public control of the city's water, a struggle against the Bolivian government and Bechtel, one of the largest global corporations. Bechtel's Bolivian subsidiary, Tenari Water (Aquas de Tenari) had a contract with the Bolivian government to privatize the water supply of Cochabamba, Bolivia's third largest city, until 2039.[1]

With the privatization agreement came Law 2029: all community water projects were now illegal; only Tenari could distribute water. Locals could not build their own wells, and water-collection tanks were banned. Local townships could no longer collect water taxes or determine where wells could be dug.[2]

Within weeks, water costs climbed 200 percent. In January 2000, *La Coordinadora* (the Coalition for the Defense of Water and Life), a coalition of local groups in and around the city with the slogan "The water is ours!," called a strike that shut down the city for three days. They continued striking when the government failed to honor earlier agreements to restore water control.[3]

Finally, on April 9, 2000, the contract with Bechtel was canceled, and Bechtel officials were removed from the country. The government turned over control to a publicly controlled water company, SEMAPA (Servicio Municipal de Agua Potable y Alcantarillado).[4] In 2004, Oscar Olivera, leader of *La Coordinadora*, wrote, "We had to 'unprivatize' the very fabric of society."[5] He said this struggle

---

1. Jim Shultz, "Bolivia: The Water War Widens," in *NACLA Report on the Americas* 36.3 (2003), 2.

2. Shultz, "Bolivia," 1; Oscar Olivera, with Tom Lewis, "The Water War," in *Cochabamba: Water War in Bolivia* (Cambridge, MA: South End Press, 2004), 9.

3. Schultz, "Bolivia," 2; Olivera, "Water War," *Cochabamba*, 30–32.

4. Schultz, "Bolivia," 2. For a discussion of SEMAPA see BNAmericas, "Water and Waste, Bolivia," *www.bnamericas.com/company-profile/en/servicio-municipal-de-agua-potable-y-alcantarillado-semapa*.

5. Olivera, "Water War," *Cochabamba*, 47. For the final resolution of the dispute, see *www.democracyctr.org/bechtel/bechtel-vs-bolivia-htm*.

meant "the reclaiming of their [Bolivians'] water as a fundamental resource," and "the reclaiming of their dignity and capacity to organize and shape their own futures themselves."[6]

Water Privatization

These stories illustrate the impact of bottled water and water privatization and highlight the differences between rainwater as a public, common good vs. water as a commodity in a global trading system. This chapter examines these choices, with an emphasis on private water and the poor.

A Little History: From the Romans to the Twenty-first Century

Since ancient times, water was not "owned" but was a community good held in public trust.[7] For example, the statutes of Roman emperor Justinian (482–518 CE) declared, "running water was held in common and could not be owned." In medieval times, residents of Foxton, near Cambridge, England, were fined "for widening or diverting the brook, trying to take more than their share of water from the common stream," while upstream villagers "had to be stopped from fouling the water with livestock."[8]

In the nineteenth century, states and municipalities, particularly in the United States and Europe, became the chief water suppliers to towns and cities due to the inability of individuals and private enterprises to meet increasing demand.[9] To this day, more than 80 percent

---

6. Aldo Orellana Lopez, "Bolivia, 15 Years on from the Water War: What Happened in Cochabamba and in Bolivia after the Water War?," Special to the *Narco News Bulletin*, April 23, 2015, *http://narconews.com/Issue67/article4799.html.*

7. Public trust doctrine emphasizes the public's right to use common resources like water. "By the law of nature these things are common to mankind, the air, running water, the sea, and consequently the shores of the sea" in "What Is the Public Trust?," *Flow: For Love of Water, http://flowforwater.org/public-trust-solutions /what-is-public-trust/.*

8. Black, *The No-nonsense Guide to Water*, 110.

9. Karen Bakker, "Archipelagos and Networks: Urbanization and Water Privatization in the South," *Geographical Journal* 169.4 (2003): 328–41, 329.

of people in the European Union and the United States are served by public agencies.[10]

However, in Latin America and Africa at the beginning of the twentieth century, cities with growing populations and large numbers of poor people were overwhelmed by demands for fresh, clean water; the supplies available could not meet this rising demand. As a result private water vendors began furnishing poor people, at a much higher cost than water delivered to the middle and upper classes, via public water systems.[11] Already water was becoming privatized, available only to those who could afford to pay. Then in the 1980s, when developing countries were unable to meet loan obligations, the World Monetary Fund and the World Bank[12] imposed new rules as conditions of obtaining more loans; the rules forced nations to open public enterprises to privatization in efforts to reduce government expenses.[13]

By the beginning of the twenty-first century, water supplies in more than one hundred cities in developing countries were controlled by large, multinational companies. Two large French companies—ONDEO/Suez Lyonaise des Eaux, now called Suez, and Vivendi/General des Eaux, renamed Viola—dominated the corporate field worldwide, owning more than 70 percent of the privatized market.[14]

Rationale for Privatization

The assumption behind privatization is that water is "a scarce commodity."[15] As an investment report in Commodity HQ notes: "Water is perhaps the most overlooked commodity in our world . . . an

10. David Hall, "Introduction," in *Reclaiming Public Water*, ed. Belen Belanya et al. (Amsterdam: Transnational Institute and Corporate Europe Observatory, 2005), 22.

11. Hall, *Reclaiming Public Water*, 22.

12. The World Bank is an international financial institution that provides loans to countries globally for capital development programs under certain conditions and rules. See World Bank, *www.worldbank.org/*.

13. Bakker, "Archipelagos and Networks," 335.

14. Maude Barlow and Tony Clarke, *Blue Gold*, 107. See also Maude Barlow and Tony Clark, "Water Privatization," Polaris Institute, January 2004, *www.globalpolicy.org/component/content/article/209/43398.html*.

15. Bakker, "Archipelagos and Networks," 335.

absolute necessity."[16] In 2011, economist Willem Buiter saw water as "an asset class that will become eventually the single most important physical-commodity-based asset class, dwarfing oil, copper, agricultural commodities and precious metals."[17] With the increasing realities of global demand exceeding supply, those favoring privatization argue that only the market can balance supply and demand because markets would give water, as it grows scarcer, a monetary value, to be bought and sold like any other commodity.[18]

For the World Bank, the remedy lies in "relaxing the government's grip," and moving from water provision as a subsidized service to water as a "tradable good and a profitable enterprise."[19] If people in poorer urban areas and poorer rural regions pay higher prices, in the eyes of the World Bank that serves as evidence of their willingness to pay higher prices.[20] The dominant ideology—that it is a good idea to import water management schemes from the industrialized world to poorer, mainly rural, areas—governs water transactions.

Water Privatization Processes

Examining water privatization, Judith Rees, vice-chair of the Grantham Research Institute on Climate Change and the Environment, London School of Economics, cites two privatization

---

16. "How to Invest in Water," CommodityHQ.com, *http://commodityhq.com/commodity/agriculture/water/*.

17. Quoted in Tom Lawson, "Reversing the Tide: Cities and Countries Are Rebelling against Water Privatization and Winning," Occupy.com, September 22, 2015, *www.occupy.com/article/reversing-tide-cities-and-countries-are-rebelling-against-water-privatization-and-winning - sthash.gCcItZEI.dpbs*.

18. Jeneen Interlandi, "The New Oil," *Newsweek*, October 18, 2010, 42.

19. Bakker, "Archipelagos and Networks," 335.

20. Department for International Development, United Kingdom, 1998 document, quoted in Bakker, "Archipelagos and Networks," 336. This was an era, which still exists today, in which privatization of energy, water, and other industries had become the economic norm. This "movement" to get governments out of the businesses of resources like water began with strong force under President Ronald Reagan and English Prime Minister Margaret Thatcher. See Daniel Yergin and Jospeh Stanislaw, *The Commanding Heights* (Free Press, 1998), updated to The *Commanding Heights: Battle for the World Economy* (New York: A Touchstone Book, 2014); also Daniel Yergin's three-part YouTube.com series, "The Commanding Heights," 2002, *www.youtube.com/watch?v=DoWbm8zUG6Y*.

methods: divestment and concession. Divestment "transfers owner-ship of infrastructure assets into private hands as well as giving the private companies responsibility for all operations, revenue raising and investment."[21] In concession, water assets technically remain public, but government "concedes" water to a private company, typi-cally for twenty-five to thirty years. The company is then responsible for management. Whether transfer or concession, Rees argues, some form of public regulation is still essential for a scarce and essential resource such as water.[22]

International Regulations

Added to the pressures of the World Bank, the World Trade Orga-nization (WTO)[23] instituted privatization through free-trade rules. The WTO's General Agreement on Trade in Services (GATS) of January 1995 focused on deregulating services such as water and opening them to trade among nations.[24] Also according to the rules of the North American Free Trade Agreement (NAFTA), water is defined as "a tradable good, obligating all levels of govern-ment . . . to sell their water resources to the highest bidder under threat of being sued by private companies."[25]

Although international investors are increasingly interested in seeing water resources become tradable, more and more major water companies are questioning existing models in serving rural areas and poor areas in major cities. Suez recently announced a reduction by up to one-third of its work in developing countries. Regarding

---

21. Judith Rees, "Regulation and Private Participation in the Water and Sanitation Sector," *TAC Background Papers* 1 (1998), 16.

22. Rees, "Regulation and Private Participation," 16, 18.

23. The WTO is "the only global international organization dealing with the rules of trade between nations." "What Is the WTO?," World Trade Organization, *www .wto.org/english/thewto_e/whatis_e/whatis_e.htm*.

24. Shiva, *Water Wars*, 96. See also *www.thirdworldtraveler.com/Water/Corp_Control _Water_VShiva.html*.

25. Jim Brown, "The Relationship between NAFTA and Canadian Water," in *The 180*, July 26, 2015, *www.cbc.ca/radio/the180/more-on-nafta-and-water-partisanship -in-government-and-should-expats-be-able-to-vote-1.3163823/the-relationship-between -nafta-and-canadian-water-1.3164244*.

water service to poor communities, the SAUR company[26] reported to the World Bank that "[t]he need far outreaches the financial and risk-taking capacities of the private sector."[27]

Results of Water Privatization

The results are mixed at best and poor, unjust, and unsustainable at worst. Prices have risen, in some cases drastically, and water quality has declined. By 2000, "In France, customer fees increased by 150 percent as a result of privatization, but water quality deteriorated."[28] In the United States, Food & Water Watch examined the water rates of the 500 largest community water systems and found that privatization of those systems resulted in a cost of $185/per year more than what local governments would charge for the same amount of water.[29]

Then in 2016 Brazil's new government imposed a privatization scheme involving a loan to help pay for the 2016 Olympic Games; the loan was contingent on the state of Rio de Janeiro selling its public water supply and sanitation system to private companies.[30]

The benefits of a market-driven commodification of water through privatization assume supply will meet demand through higher pricing, resulting in lower consumption. However, there is a high price to pay. A commodity is sold to the highest bidder, not to those who need it most. Companies privatizing water can charge whatever the market will bear and may spend little on maintenance and environmental needs. In fact, private companies have little

---

26. SAUR is an international corporation involved in water supply and wastewater treatment service. See SAUR at *www.saur.com/en/*.

27. Quoted in Black, *No-nonsense*, 79.

28. Vandana Shiva, "World Bank, WTO, and Corporate Control Over Water," *International Socialist Review* (August-September 2001), 41.

29. "Water Privatization: Facts and Figures," Food and Water Watch, August 31, 2015, *www.foodandwaterwatch.org/insight/water-privatization-facts-and-figures*. See *www.ft.com/content/91a2779a-4077-11e7-9d56-25f963e998b2* for a 2017 story by the University of Greenwich of a similar increase of prices in England.

30. Corporate Europe Observatory, "Brazil's New Government Imposes Rio Water Privatization to Pay for Olympic Games," Global Research, July 14, 2016, *www.globalresearch.ca/brazils-new-government-imposes-rio-water-privatization-to-pay-for-olympic-games/5537272*.

incentive to move toward conservation measures because revenues drop when customers conserve.[31]

Resistance to Water Privatization

Resistance to water privatization is growing. In October 2004, Uruguayans approved by 64.6 percent a "constitutional reform that defines water as a good belonging to the public trust and guarantees civil society's participation in the management of the country's hydrological resources." Voters agreed that public management of water should rest on the criteria of public participation and sustainability; private provisions for water were illegal.[32]

Resistance to water privatization by corporations is on the rise globally, as people struggle to obtain good, clean water for families, animals, and crops.

---

31. Interlandi, "The New Oil," *Newsweek*, 42, 48. For more discussion on the impacts of water privatization, see Christine Gudorf and James Huchingson, "Water: Economic Commodity and Divine Gift," in *Boundaries: A Casebook in Environmental Ethics*, 2nd ed. (Washington, DC: Georgetown University Press, 2010), 121–41; and John Vidal, "Water Privatisation: A Worldwide Failure?," *The Guardian*, January 30, 2015, *www.theguardian.com/global-development/2015/jan/30/water-privatisation-worldwide-failure-lagos-world-bank*.

32. Carlos Santos and Albert Villarreal, "Uruguay: Victorious Social Struggle for Water," in *Reclaiming Public Water*, 173, 178–79.

In 2009, Camden, New Jersey, sued United Water, a subsidiarity of Suez, "for $29 million in unapproved payments, high unaccounted for water losses, poor maintenance, and service disruptions."[33] Cities across the United States are buying back public control of their privatized water systems—for example, Atlanta, Georgia, and Hoboken, New Jersey. The process of "remunicipalization" is also growing around the world.[34] In 2012, the European Commission announced formal antitrust proceedings against Veolia, Suez, and SAUR; the issues centered on collusion in prices to consumers.[35] In 2014, Paris returned its water services to public ownership.[36] In a 2014 report, the Transnational Institute noted that some 180 cities in thirty-five countries have reversed private water contracts and handed back control of the water supply to municipalities in the prior fifteen years.[37] In April 2016, US Representative Gwen Moore, Wisconsin, raised concerns about the World Bank's role in promoting water privatization. In a letter to World Bank president, Jim Yong Kim, Moore argued the bank's lending arm had not adequately monitored the conflicts of interest created when it took a stake in water corporations.[38]

Bottled Water

Bottled water might not seem like water privatization. However, as the story about the student trip to Belize shows, bottled water is a

33. Interlandi, "The New Oil," *Newsweek*, 44.

34. Joseph Erbentraut, "There's a Secret War Being Waged over Your Drinking Water," *Huffington Post*, December 21, 2015, *www.huffingtonpost.com/entry/water -privatization-why-you-should-care_us_5671cb10e4b0648fe301fab2.*

35. Stefanie Spear, "France Shows Why Water Privatization Is a Bad Idea," Eco-Watch, January 20, 2016, *www.ecowatch.com/france-shows-why-water-privatization -is-a-bad-idea-1881573729.html.*

36. "Paris's Return to Public Water Supplies Makes Waves beyond France," *Reuters*, July 8, 2014, *https://in.reuters.com/article/water-utilities-paris/pariss-return-to-public -water-supplies-makes-waves-beyond-france-idINL6N0PE57220140708.*

37. Lawson, "Reversing the Tide," *www.occupy.com/article/reversing-tide-cities-and -countries-are-rebelling-against-water-privatization-and-winning#sthash.gCcItZEI .dpbs.* See also "Privatization Watch," Public Services International, March 2017, for an update on efforts from around the world to resist privatization of water supply and sanitation. *www.world-psi.org/en/privatization-watch-032017.*

38. Sarah Jerome, "Top Congresswoman Questions Public-Private Water Deals," *Water Online*, April 16, 2016, *www.wateronline.com/doc/top-congresswoman-questions -public-private-water-deals-0001.*

commodity for the privileged. There are exceptions, such as the use of bottled water in emergencies, as was the case during the water crisis in Flint, Michigan,[39] and during times of health concerns in countries with polluted, impure water.

Yet as water quality deteriorates, world bottlers "target their 'pure water' to specialty, i.e. economically advantaged, audiences: 'Water for sportsmen and sportswomen, water for pregnant women, water for babies, water for growing children—all part of the contribution of bottled water to perfect health at every age and in all circumstances.'"[40]

History of Bottled Water

Bottled water arrived in the United States in 1978 as a result of mass-marketing by Perrier.[41] Since then, bottled water sales have risen dramatically worldwide, led by Pepsi, Coke, and Nestlé. Clever marketing of bottled water as "pure water" taps into consumer desire for a healthy lifestyle. Yet Coke's Dasani brand and Pepsi's Aquafina are no more than tap water that has been purified and filtered. Water from icebergs off the coast of Svalbard, Norway, has made its way to Harrods of London in bottles selling for £80 (approximately $100 US) each.[42]

Nestlé has been particularly aggressive in building bottling plants in the United States. In 2008, with promises of jobs, Nestlé Waters Northwest attempted to build a bottling plant in the small town of Enumclaw, Washington, southeast of Seattle. The plant would have used some one hundred million gallons a year from a

---

39. Flint residents have been forced to use bottled water until their water for drinking, cooking, bathing, and other uses is declared safe. The average number of standard-size (16.9-ounce) bottles needed to cook and clean daily for a family of three in Flint is sixty. Rachael Feltman, "Flint: A Day by the Bottle," *Popular Science*, March–April 2017, 11.

40. Ricardo Petralla, *The Water Manifesto* (London: Zed Books, 2001), 80–82.

41. Annie Shuppy, "Prime Numbers, H2OU," *The Chronicle of Higher Education*, L3, No. 11 (November 3, 2006): A7.

42. Katherine Purvis, "'Luxury Water' for £80 a Bottle? It's Ignorant, Insensitive and Irresponsible," *Guardian*, February 15, 2017, *www.theguardian.com /global-development-professionals-network/2017/feb/15/luxury-water-for-80 =-a-bottle-its-ignorant-inssnsitive-and-irresponsible.*

nearby underground spring. However, the city declined Nestlé's request based on concerns about water availability and on principle about public welfare versus corporate power. Another Nestlé proposal met a similar fate in the town of Orting, Washington.[43]

In September 2009, due to strong opposition from locals and indigenous communities, Nestlé scrapped plans to build the largest US water bottling facility in McCloud, California.[44] In Oregon, Cascade Locks County voters fought a Nestlé proposal for a bottling plant and banned commercial water bottling in 2016. The struggle reveals how easy it is for a major company with money and lawyers to move around town by town.[45]

The Problems with Bottled Water

There are some major problems with producing bottled water:

1. Producing the bottles uses seventeen million barrels of oil a year, not including transportation.[46]
2. US consumers in 2015 used more than fifty billion water bottles, but according to the Container Recycling Institute, some 86 percent of plastic water bottles used in the United States ended up in landfills.[47]

Continued

---

43. Cara Solomon, "Nestlé Water Plant? Not in Our Town, Enumclaw Says," *Seattle Times*, October 7, 2008, A1, A9.

44. "Nestlé Sent Packing from McCloud." *In Action: Corporate Accountability International* (Fall 2009): 1, 3.

45. Olga Kreimer, "A Water-bottling Plant Creates a Rift in Montana," *https://www.hcn.org/articles/water-a-water-bottle-plant-raises-the-specter-of-development-in-montanas-flathead-valley*.

46. "Bottled Water and Energy Fact Sheet," The Pacific Institute, February 2007, *http://pacinst.org/publication/bottled-water-and-energy-a-fact-sheet/*.

47. Hannah Ellsbury, "Plastic Water Bottles Impose Health and Environmental Risks," Ban the Bottle, August 23, 2012, *www.banthebottle.net/articles/plastic-water-bottles-impose-health-and-environmental-risks/*. Unless otherwise indicated, the source for the information is in note 45.

The Problems with Bottled Water *continued*

---

3. The per capita consumption of bottled water amounted to 39.3 gallons in 2016.[48]

4. In the United States plastic bottles create 2.7 billion pounds of landfill garbage per year.[49]

5. In the United States, one in five states has no regulations for water use for bottled water "made" in their state.

6. No requirements exist banning *E coli* or fecal matter in bottled water in the United States.[50]

Environmental Impact

Bottled water draws down water levels, thereby reducing water essential for healthy vegetation and for healthy bird and animal populations. By using large amounts of fossil fuel in its manufacture and transport, bottled water contributes significantly to global warming.

Quality, Safety

Contrary to popular belief, bottled water may not be any purer than tap water. In 1999, after a four-year study testing 103 water brands, the Natural Resources Defense Council concluded that, "there is no assurance that just because water comes out of a bottle . . . it is any cleaner or safer than water from the tap. In fact, an estimated 25 to 40 percent of bottled water really is tap water in a bottle— sometimes further treated, sometimes not."[51]

---

48. "Per Capita Consumption of Bottled Water per Year in the United States from 1999 to 2016 (in gallons)," The Statistics Portal, *www.statista.com/statistics/183377 /per-capita-consumption-of-bottled-water-in-the-us-since-1999/*.

49. "Bottled Water and Energy Fact Sheet," *http://pacinst.org/publication/bottled -water-and-energy-a-fact-sheet/*.

50. Bryan Walsh, "Back to the Tap," *Time*, August 9, 2007; "The High Price of Bottled Water," *The Week*, September 7, 2007, *www.google.com/search?q=bottled +water+use+per+year&rlz=1C1CHWA_enUS557US557&oq=bottled+water+use+per +year&aqs=chrome..69i57j0.12192j0j8&sourceid=chrome&ie=UTF-8*.

51. Cameron Woodworth, "A Clean Drink of Water," *PCC Sound Consumer*, August 2004, 4.

Also increased reliance on bottled water translates into less attention spent on keeping public water clean. Yearly, ten million gallons of sewage flow through taps, sickening more than nineteen million people. The EPA believes that more than $300 billion is needed to fix such systems.[52]

Last, public water is monitored several times daily by the EPA, with tight restrictions, whereas bottled water monitored by the Food and Drug Administration (FDA) is only tested weekly. Nor does the FDA require public disclosure of sources, treatment processes, and any contaminants found; the EPA requires that all this information be disclosed to residents yearly.[53]

Costs

Compared with tap water, which costs an average of nineteen cents a day, an equal amount of bottled water costs as much as $4.98 per day.[54] *Business Insider* estimated in 2013 that bottled water costs two thousand times as much as tap water.[55]

Alternatives to Bottled Water

For those looking to reduce their use of bottled water, here are three options:

- Refillable water bottles—filling with tap water saves hundreds of dollars a year.

Continued

---

52. McKay Coppins, "Water Woes, and Not Just in New Mexico," *Newsweek*, October 4, 2010, 6.

53. Sanaz Majd, "Should You Drink Tap or Bottled Water?," *Scientific American*, October 21, 2015, *www.scientificamerican.com/articleshould-you-drink-tap-or-bottled-water/*.

54. Bryan Walsh, "Back to the Tap," *Time*, August 9, 2007.

55. Matthew Bosler, "Bottled Water Costs 2000 Times as Much as Tap Water," *Business Insider*, July 12, 2013, *www.businessinsider.com/bottled-water-costs-2000x-more-than-tap-2013-7*.

> **Alternatives to Bottled Water** *continued*
> _____
>
> - Water carafes—filters water and costs about thirty-one cents per gallon.
> - Under-sink filter system—filters water and costs around forty-two cents per gallon.[56]

Banning the Bottle

By 2016, "Ban the Bottle" campaigns led more than seventy-five colleges and universities in the United States and Canada to ban bottled water on campus,[57] including such schools as the University of Toronto, Canada, in 2010, and Drake University, Des Moines, Iowa, in 2013. In 2017 students at the University of California, San Diego, undertook a similar campaign; the "All Campuses Plastic Water Bottle Ban" campaign hopes to implement lasting policy not only at UC San Diego, but also at all University of California campuses.[58] In April 2017 the University of Hong Kong became the first university in Hong Kong to ban bottled water on campus.[59]

At my own campus, Seattle University, students too led the "Ban the Bottle" campaign over a three-year period, holding water tasting contests (sponsored by Corporate Accountability), fostering topic panels, gathering signatures on petitions, undertaking research papers,[60] and addressing the university's board of trustees. Despite a fear of lost

_____

56. Gary Chamberlain, "Ten Reasons Not to Buy Bottled Water," handout for the author's theology class, "Religion and Ecology," 2013.

57. "Ban the Bottle, Map of Campaign," *www.banthebottle.net.*

58. "Student Campaign for a Bottled Water-free University of Toronto a Success," CISION, August 26, 2011, *www.newswire.ca/news-releases/student-campaign-for-a -bottled-water-free-university-of-toronto-a-success-508694791.html*; Jens Manuel Krogstad, "Student-led Campaign at Drake Cans Bottled Water Sales," *USA TODAY*, April 8, 2013, *www.usatoday.com/story/news/nation/2013/04/08/bottled-water-sales-ban-drake /2065273/*; Deborah Jude, "Students Seek to Ban Plastic Water Bottles from Campus," May 1, 2017, *https://phys.org/news/2017-05-students-plastic-bottles-campus.html.*

59. Hannah Ellsbury, "Hong Kong University Takes the Lead to Ban Bottled Water," Ban the Bottle, April 21, 2017, *www.banthebottle.net/articles/hong-kong -unveristy-takes-the-lead-to-ban-bottled-water/.*

60. Brandon Knight and Kevin Brown, "A Proposal for the Seattle University Administration Regarding the Sale of Bottled Water on Campus," June 10, 2009.

revenue, the university administration canceled the contract with Pepsi for its Aquafina brand, installed spigots to fill water bottles, and promoted a bottled-water–free campus, the first among West Coast schools.

In addition, several cities have moved to ban bottled water on city-owned property and at city-sponsored events. For example, in 2013, Concord, Massachusetts, with seventeen thousand residents, became the first city in America to ban the sale of single-use plastic water bottles. San Francisco initiated a four-year phaseout that began in 2014. By 2017 more than one hundred cities in the United States had enacted measures to restrict government spending on bottled water, and bans had also spread to national parks.[61] However, the Trump administration has since rescinded the ban in national parks,[62] in spite of a report from the National Park Service that the ban worked in reducing plastic bottle waste," saving "up to two million water bottles" per year.[63]

Catholic Social Teaching Responds

The principle of a right to public water clashes with water as a commodity for sale for private gain. In the latter calculus, water becomes a product, available only to those able to pay. At this point, an examination of CST builds upon principles and arguments developed in previous chapters. Fundamentally for CST water is a "public" good, part of the goods of creation, fundamental to life; also governments—local, state, national—have obligations to provide people with access to safe, drinkable water.

61. Sam Levin, "How San Francisco Is Leading the Way out of Bottled Water Culture," *The Guardian*, June 28, 2017, *www.theguardian.com/environment/2017/jun/28/how-san-francisco-is-leading-the-way-out-of-bottled-water-culture*; Darryl Fears, "National Parks Put a Ban on Bottled Water to Ease Pollution. Trump Just Sided with the Lobby That Fought It," *Washington Post*, August 17, 2017, *www.washingtonpost.com/news/energy-environment/wp/2017/08/17/national-parks-banned-bottled-water-to-ease-pollution-trump-just-sided-with-the-lobby-that-fought-it/?*.

62. Allison Aubrey, "Trump Administration Reverses Bottled Water Ban in National Parks," National Public Radio, August 18, 2017, *www.npr.org/sections/thesalt/2017/08/18/544456726/trump-administration-reverses-bottled-water-ban-in-national-parks*.

63. Daryll Fears, "The National Park Service Showed That Its Bottled Water Ban Worked—Then Lifted It," *The Washington Post*, September 26, 2017, *www.washingtonpost.com/news/energy-environment/wp/2017/09/26/the-national-park-service-showed-that-its-bottled-water-ban-worked-then-lifted-it/?utm_term=.6a8c6950*.

Popes John XXIII, Paul VI, and John Paul II

In his 1961 encyclical *Mater et magistra (Christianity and Social Progress)*, John XXIII used the principle of the common good to speak to the "conditions of human living," which involve "principal services needed by all," including "pure drinking water" (*MM* 127). In 1963 in *Pacem in terris (Peace on Earth)*, he argued that governments must pay "attention to the development of such essential services as water supply" (*PT* 64). In his 1967 encyclical *Populorum progressio (On the Development of Peoples)*, Paul VI reframed the discussion in terms of the universal destination of human goods; although he does not mention water specifically, it is one of those "goods" for all (*PP* 22–23).

Then Pope John Paul II, in his 1987 encyclical *Sollicitudo rei socialis (On Social Concern)*, referred to the "availability of drinking water" as a key indicator of justice in relation to common goods (*SRS* 10, 28). Finally, in *Centesimus annus (On the Hundredth Anniversary of Rerum novarum)* in 1991, John Paul II clarified the role of the state in the case of public goods such as water: "It is the task of the state to provide for the defense and preservation of common goods such as the natural and human environments, which cannot be safeguarded simply by market forces" (CA 40).

Pope Benedict XVI: *Caritas in veritate* (*Charity in Truth*)

In *Caritas in veritate* (*Charity in Truth*), Benedict XVI's primary concern is that economic activities have as their goal the distribution of Earth's goods—such as water—to all peoples, especially the poor: "The environment is God's gift to everyone, and in our use of it we have a responsibility towards the poor, towards future generations and towards humanity as a whole" (*CV* 48).

Benedict XVI warns that the "hoarding of resources, especially water," can generate "serious conflicts among the peoples involved" (*CV* 51). The ethical challenge lies in cultivating "a public conscience that considers food and access to water as universal rights of all human beings, without distinction" (*CV* 27). Water privatization and bottled water practices fail that challenge.

Pope Francis, *Laudato si'*: On Care for Our Common Home

Francis echoes many of Benedict XVI's themes, such as promotion of the common good and a special concern for the poor, and introduces the plight of indigenous peoples. Francis is especially concerned about the depletion of natural resources and an unsustainable "level of consumption in developed countries and wealthier sectors of society, where the habit of wasting and discarding has reached unprecedented levels" (*LS* 27). He writes that water shortages have occurred in various parts of the world, and great disparities exist: "Some countries have areas rich in water while others endure drastic scarcity" (*LS* 28).

Throughout his writings, Francis is concerned with the plight of the poor. Good water quality is often not available to the poor, leading to "the spread of water-related diseases," and even death (*LS* 29). Given the diminishing supply of fresh, clean, uncontaminated water, Francis warns against "turning it into a commodity subject to the laws of the market." On the contrary, Francis asserts that access to safe, drinkable water "is a basic and universal human right, essential to human survival, and a condition for the exercise of other human rights." Concerning privatization, Francis notes "that the control of water by large multinational businesses may become a major source of conflict in this century" (*LS* 30–31).

Precedents to Papal Statements

John Allen, an international correspondent for several Catholic magazines, has written an important article that indicates the extent to which many bishops' conferences around the world as well as Catholic organizations have articulated important principles of CST in relation to the environment and water. In relation to water privatization, for example, he notes the work of the Brazilian bishops as far back as 2006: "the Catholic Conference of Bishops in Brazil affirmed a 'human right to water' and to a safe environment, and expressed support for community-based alternatives to water privatization."[64]

---

64. John L. Allen, "If *Laudato Si'* Is an Earthquake, It Had Plenty of Early Tremors," *Crux*, June 18, 2015, *https://cruxnow.com/church/2015/06/18/if-laudato-si -is-an-earthquake-it-had-plenty-of-early-tremors/*.

Principles at Work

These encyclicals and statements provide a powerful set of principles for analysis of the use, distribution, and availability of water as an essential part of the common good. The arguments promote an understanding that water is not for the self-interests of particular groups, such as corporations and states; local people must be integrally involved in access to and the distribution, pricing, and sale of water.

In addition to grounding the essential nature of water as a public good, several other principles operate here. One is sustainability, which provides governments with a key question—namely, do current practices and policies ensure not only a sufficient quantity and quality of water today but also a sufficient quantity and quality in the future? The solution for a population's need for potable water lies not in buying bottled water, an unsustainable solution, but in providing ways to ensure sufficient amounts of drinkable water in public supplies.

Equally important are the principles of subsidiarity and accountability. Through privatization, local control is transferred to large corporate powers driven by profit motives and with little accountability. The struggles in Cochabamba reveal that without such accountability to the public at large, injustice occurs. In the case of private companies, prices may be raised beyond the ability of the poorest to pay, with less assurance of quality.[65]

In addition, the principles of equality and participation assert that every human has a right to potable water. Measures that overuse such a scarce resource for the benefit of a few violate equality. Participation dictates that those affected by a decision may participate in that decision and are represented by an agency acting on behalf of their interests.

Conclusion

Water must be understood as an essential public good, required for the common good not just of humans but also of all creatures and of Earth itself, in order to promote the flourishing of all. From this perspective, privatization by government concession or divestment would not be a sustainable model. At the same time, governments

---

65. See Shiva, *Water Wars*, for an incisive discussion of the impacts of water privatization by large companies.

struggle to keep up with demand for water and often lack the financial resources to meet those demands. Cooperation with private corporations and entrepreneurs may sometimes seem essential, although when governments concede water rights, key ethical questions arise around basic rights to common goods, public accountability, participation, subsidiarity, and equity. In future discussions of water as a public good, the place of regulations—democratic, accountable, with public oversight—of water, both as a scarce resource and as a public good, to ensure sustainable water use is a key to just policies.

As Benedict XVI warns in *Caritas in veritate*, "While the poor of the world continue knocking on the doors of the rich, the world of affluence runs the risk of no longer hearing those knocks, on account of a conscience that can no longer distinguish what is human" (*CV* 75).

Review Questions

1. What are the advantages of privatization?
2. What are the disadvantages of privatization?
3. What types of privatization are most commonly used?
4. What alternatives to bottled water exist for those concerned about tap water purity?
5. What new arguments against privatization do you find in the CST writings?

Discussion Questions

1. What types of regulations would you recommend if water were to be privatized?
2. Under what conditions would you justify the privatization of water?
3. Do you or your family and friends drink bottled water? How much and how often? Why?
4. What are the strongest CST arguments for or against privatization and bottled water? What are the weaknesses of the CST approach?
5. Would you argue for or against state subsidies for water in order for to all citizens to have access to it? Why?

CHAPTER

The Right to Water

The one opinion, which I think is extreme, is represented by the NGOs [nongovernmental organizations] who bang on about declaring water a public right. That means as a human being you should have a right to water. That's an extreme solution.[1]

—Peter Brabeck, Chairman of the Board,
Nestlé Corporation

If we can determine that water is a right, it gives citizens a tool they can use against their governments. If you believe it is a human right, then you believe that you can't refuse to give it to someone because they can't afford it.[2]

—Maude Barlow, senior adviser on water issues
to the president of the UN General Assembly

The Water Conundrum

These statements reflect the current conundrum of water scarcity, purity, and access: is water a basic right or is it a commodity? Can it be both? CST often says there is a human right to water, because

---

1. Quoted in "Nestlé's Water Privatization Push," in *The Story of Stuff Project*, *http://action.storyofstuff.org/sign/nestle_water_privatization_push.* Brabeck has since backtracked on his statement, but Nestlé Corporation has not.

2. Quoted in Yigal Schleifer, "Is Access to Clean Water a Basic Human Right?," in *Christian Science Monitor*, March 19, 2009, *http://www.csmonitor.com/2009/0319 /p06s01-woeu.html.*

it is essential to life and is, indeed, the foundation upon which other rights rest. Nonetheless, it is important to examine the basis itself for the human right to water, both in international documents and in Catholic social teaching.

Rights: What Are They?

A dictionary lists several definitions for a *right* that get at the core of "a right to water." One meaning, for example, defines *right* as "a just claim or title, whether legal, prescriptive or moral." The next meaning listed for *right* says it is "a moral, ethical, or legal principle considered as an underlying cause of truth, justice, morality, or ethics."[3] A right could then be termed a moral or legal claim or demand made on an entity (such as a government) based on a notion of what it means to be a person. Pope John Paul II noted in his 1991 encyclical *Centesimus annus* (*On the Hundredth Anniversary of Rerum novarum*) that in addition to political rights and social and economic rights that are derived from membership in a national state, there are fundamental rights "which flow from one's essential dignity as a person" (*CA* 11).

In response, the individuals or groups against whom the claim is made have an obligation to ensure, as far as possible, that a right can be exercised. The right to vote, for example, is a legal right one has as a citizen, and it can be revoked by public authority, as in the case of someone convicted of a felony. At the same time, states have an obligation to promote the full exercise of a right. Rights such as the right to water that are so fundamental to what it means to be human apply universally.

Water Rights: Historical Guidance

In the early days of the United States, and especially during westward expansion, rules guiding access to water in rivers and streams emerged. These rules, called "riparian rights" (*ripa* in Latin means "bank" of a river) recognized the rights of various communities living

---

3. Definition of *right*, *Random House Compact Unabridged Dictionary* (New York: Random House, 1987), 1656.

along the banks of rivers to withdraw water from the flow, provided they did no damage to other users. This principle dominated in the wet, rain-blessed states east of the Mississippi River. Today, eastern states still use the principle of riparian rights: communities near rivers and streams can make reasonable withdrawals, and individuals do not "own" water. However, in the arid western states, in particular in the Southwest, great water battles[4] have been waged on the rule of "prior appropriation": the first one at the river or stream gets the first claim; the second one gets the second claim, and so on, producing a system of senior rights and junior rights. Originally, the Resnicks (see chapter 4, "Water Scarcity for Most and Abundance for Few"), for example, only held junior water rights. To gain rights to water, they bought water rights from senior water-rights holders with no state oversight. Water rights in California are the property of the holder. Yet even in such cases, the rights are to the use of the water, not ownership.[5]

The principle of prior appropriation also holds that one's water rights, in any given year, are only equal to the amount of water used in the previous year. What emerges from this is a "use it or lose it" mentality.[6] There is little incentive to conserve, because less use in any one-year cycle means the holder of the water right loses that amount in the next cycle. Yet even where eastern-style "riparian rights" still hold, the state government owns the water in its jurisdiction and makes final decisions on water use for water-rights holders.

At the beginning of the twenty-first century, as clean water became more prized and competition for water more acute, water had been identified as a "scarce resource" and a "commodity" to be traded. With most of the world's freshwater channeled by dams, canals, pipes,

---

4. For a look at western water wars, particularly the southwestern United States, see Marc Reisner's classic, *Cadillac Desert*. For a visual story, see Roman Polanski's 1974 film, *Chinatown*, inspired by the struggle to supply water to the rapidly expanding city of Los Angeles.

5. Prior appropriation originated during the California Gold Rush of the mid eighteenth century. Miners who needed water for their operations on public land used the same rule for water as for minerals: "first in time, first in right." See Elizabeth Arnold, "The Battle over Water Rights: In the West, the Oldest Claims Take Precedence," *National Public Radio*, August 28, 2003, *www.npr.org/programs/atc/features/2003/aug/water/part3.html*.

6. Sandra Postel and Brian Richter, *Rivers for Life: Managing Water for People and Nature* (Washington, DC: Island Press, 2003), 93–94.

and other means, the owners of these structures have come to assert greater control, often seen as "ownership," over the water itself.

By the 1980s, the failure of public authorities to deliver and guarantee adequate freshwater and sanitation in many parts of the world ushered in our current era of privatization, that is, corporate, private ownership, based on principles of economic exchange. At question is, "if people who, for centuries, have used the waters of a given river to support their lives and livelihoods do not 'own' it, then how can a company with a license from the state exclude them and behave as if it does?"[7]

Outlook of Private Companies

Even private companies, despite the controversies they faced surrounding privatization, support the right to water. "Our industry supports the right to water," says Gerard Payen, former adviser on Water and Sanitation to the UN secretary general, and honorary president at AquaFed, an international federation of two hundred private water operators operating in more than thirty countries. "But we are practitioners, and as practitioners, we know that proclaiming the right to water is not enough. Our job is to deliver water to people."[8] Maude Barlow, senior adviser on water issues to the president of the UN General Assembly, argues that, although there is a proper role for "the private sector to help us secure our water future," there must also be recognition that "water is a public trust. It's not the market that should decide who has access to water. It should be a public trust and a public right."[9]

The Outlook in the United States

Nowhere in the US Declaration of Independence or the Bill of Rights of the Constitution is there mention of a human right to water. Cass Sunstein, a Harvard law professor, argues that President Franklin D. Roosevelt's New Deal programs of the 1930s, which recognized

---

7. Black, *No-nonsense*, 117, 119.

8. Schleifer, "Is Access to Clean Water a Basic Human Right?"

9. Quoted in Schleifer, "Is Access to Clean Water a Basic Human Right?"

a government obligation to provide a basic standard of living, represented a second Bill of Rights. Suffolk University law professor Sharmila Murphy writes that clean drinking water belongs in this collection of rights, as evidenced in state and federal laws, such as the Clean Water Act and Safe Drinking Water Act, among others.[10]

The people of Flint certainly believe in such a right and a government obligation to support that right. In fact, as far back as 2014, the UN special assistant for research and reporting for the human right to safe drinking water maintained that by shutting off water to poor African American families, the city of Detroit had neglected the obligation to fulfill citizens' water rights without discrimination.[11]

Global Recognitions

Nations, too, have ruled on the right to water. The South African constitution of 1996, written after apartheid was overthrown, guarantees access to "sufficient clean water" as a basic right, which has allowed individuals to take legal action when their water has been cut off. A 1998 South African water law states that meeting minimum human needs with a reserve of water has first claim on the country's water resources. South African courts have determined that every household must be provided with a minimum of six thousand liters (1,585 gallons) of water per month, even if they cannot afford it.[12] Here, again, the right to water and an obligation of government to provide households with water are recognized.

After South Africa's early actions on water, other countries have taken similar measures. Cities and nations have fought to secure the grounding of a right to water in specific principles and policies. The people of Uruguay, for example, voted to amend their constitution to secure a right to water. Citizens in Grenoble, France, claim, "Water, it should be a right for all."[13] In Cali, Colombia, Hildebrando Velez,

---

10. Brian Palmer, "Is Water a Human Right?" Natural Resources Defense Council, March 3, 2016, *www.nrdc.org/onearth/water-human-right.*

11. Ibid.

12. Ibid.

13. Raymond Avrillier, "A Return to the Source: Re-Municipalisation of Water Services in Grenoble, France," in *Reclaiming Public Water*, ed. Belen Balanya et al. (Amsterdam: Transnational Institute and Corporate Europe Observatory, 2005), 65.

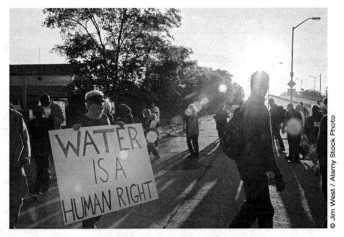

Water is not only an important resource but also is now seen as a basic human right, fundamental to the exercise of all other rights. People who care about water express that demand around the globe.

ecologist and director of CENSAT (National Center of Health, Environment, and Work), writes, "Services [water and sanitation] must be considered . . . the fundamental right of every person."[14] Tobias Schmitz, a water resources expert with Both Ends, a Dutch environmental and development organization, notes the difficulty around establishing such a legal right: "Everybody is grappling with the issue, knowing that we need to secure this right. But the question now is over the practical application of this right."[15]

The United Nations

Given the many twentieth-century documents on human rights, it may be surprising that as late as the 1990s there were no explicit documents asserting a basic human right to water. Indeed, this right was not included in the UN's 1948 Universal Declaration of Human Rights.[16]

---

14. Hildebrando Velez, "Public Services in Colombia: A Matter of Democracy," in *Reclaiming Public Water*, 103.

15. Schleifer, "Is Access to Clean Water a Basic Human Right?"

16. United Nations General Assembly, *Universal Declaration of Human Rights*, General Assembly Resolution 217A, December 10, 1948, *www.un.org/en/universal-declaration-human-rights/*.

The UN Conference on the Environment and Development, held in Rio de Janeiro in 1992, established the concept of sustainable development in relation to water and led to the institution of World Water Day, held annually on March 22. In the same year, the World Bank worked with UN agencies to establish the World Water Council, which sponsors the industry-led World Water Forum, funded by the world's large water companies.[17]

Finally, in November 2002, the UN Committee on Economic, Social and Cultural Rights explicitly affirmed a right to water and obligated governments to "progressively extend access to sufficient, affordable, accessible and safe water supplies and to safe sanitation services."[18] Also in 2002, the preparation committee of the World Summit on Sustainable Development at Johannesburg directly linked poverty eradication and water, a major step in linking "poverty eradication, water management, and health and social structures of countries."[19]

In the 2006 UN World Water Development Report 2, a right to water is carefully defined as "authorized demands to use (part of) a flow of surface water and groundwater, . . . among which a key element is the power to take part in collective decision-making about system management and direction."[20] Yet this document addresses only drinking water, not water for other needs. These statements were important preparations for the future, but a clear statement regarding a universal human right to water was still missing.

On July 26, 2010, however, the UN General Assembly passed a resolution to ensure a basic human right to safe and clean drinking water and sanitation. Then in September, the UN Human Rights Council further affirmed that a right to water and sanitation is legally binding. Governments now have binding obligations to make certain a right to water is exercised. Catarina de

---

17. Riccardo Petrella, *The Water Manifesto* (London: Zed Books, 2001), 25–27.

18. "A Right to Water: A Step in the Right Direction," WaterAid, *www.wateraid.org.uk/*, quoted in Black, *No-nonsense*, 121; United Nations, *Water: A Shared Responsibility, the United Nations World Water Development Report 2* (New York: Berghahn Books, 2006), 63.

19. Quoted in United Nations, *Water for People, Water for Life*, 28, 20–21.

20. United Nations, *Water: A Shared Responsibility*, 61. This UN report takes its definition from L. Beccar et al., "Water Rights and Collective Action in Community," in *Water Rights and Empowerment*, ed. Rutgerd Boelens and Paul Hoogendam (Assen, The Netherlands: Gorcum, 2002).

Albuquerque, the UN independent expert on human rights obligations, states, "The right to water and sanitation is a human right, equal to all other human rights, which implies that it is justiciable and enforceable."[21] That means a right to water can be adjudicated in court and that an obligation to enforce this right exists for all governments.

However, the United States was not one of the 122 nations to affirm this statement. Instead, the United States joined forty-one other UN members, including Canada, China, and other developed countries, such as Spain, France, Japan, and the United Kingdom, in abstaining—in not recognizing a universal human right to water. Perhaps one large concern is the misconception that adopting such a universal right would require water-rich countries to share their water with other countries.[22] However, in implementing this right, countries only have to do their best to provide water, in a "progressive realization." A government doing its best, given the resources available to it, but failing to supply freshwater for citizens is not considered in violation of citizens' human rights or the UN mandate.[23] Certainly, a major concern involves enforcement: if there is a human right to water, how does a government fulfill its obligation to meet that right? This question remains a point of contention among rich and poor countries worldwide.

Rui Veras, communications officer for the International Water Association (IWA), comments that since the 2010 UN declaration of the right to water, "important progress has been made in terms of policy formulation, legislation and regulation. In an increasing number of countries, these rights are being enshrined in national Constitutions." The IWA has developed guidelines for how to implement the right to water and sanitation into policies.[24]

---

21. "Human Right to Water," *Amos*, Fall 2010, 5; Intercommunity Peace and Justice Center, "Right to Water and Sanitation Is Legally Binding," *NewsCenter*, October 1, 2010, *www.unwater.org/UN News Service*.

22. Schleifer, "Is Access to Clean Water a Basic Human Right?"

23. Palmer, "Is Water a Human Right?"

24. Rui Veras, "Manual of the Human Rights to Safe Drinking Water and Sanitation for Practitioners," in IWA, March 17, 2017, *www.iwa-network.org/video /manual-of-the-human-rights-to-safe-drinking-water-and-sanitation-for-practitioners/*.

CST and the Right to Water

The tradition of CST asserts that a basic right to water exists and that the primary role of government is to ensure water is accessible to all. These principles rest upon the philosophical/theological base of an ethic rooted in the common good, human dignity, and equal rights. Governments serve the common good of the community and safeguard the basic dignity of persons and their entitlements to the goods of the created world. Water is a gift from the Creator to all.

Pope John XXIII in his 1961 encyclical *Mater et magistra* (*Christianity and Social Progress*) included "pure drinking water" as part of the conditions of social living and the "principal services needed by all" (*MM* 127). In his 1963 encyclical, *Pacem in terris* (*Peace on Earth*), John XXIII asserts that the goal of government is "the realization of the common good" in which all members of the state are "entitled to share"; the state then is to "give wholehearted and careful attention . . . to the development . . . of such essential services as water supply" (*PT* 64).

Pope Paul VI, in his 1967 encyclical, *Populorum progressio* (*On the Development of Peoples*), elaborates on the universal destination of human goods, which includes a right to water. He continues, "All other rights whatsoever, including those of property and of free commerce ["free trade" in another translation] are to be subordinated to this principle" (*PP* 22–23).

Pope John Paul II reiterated these principles of the universal destination of human goods, such as drinking water in *Sollicitudo rei socialis* (*On Social Concern*), 1987 (*SRS* 10), and the priority of access to such goods over the interests of private ownership in *Laborem exercens* (*On Human Work*), 1981 (*LE* 14). Finally in *Centesimus annus* (On the Hundredth Anniversary of *Rerum novarum*), 1991, he argues that it is the state's obligation to safeguard and protect these goods, which involve the natural and human environment, ensuring that water is available to all (*CA* 40).

Pontifical Council for Justice and Peace at the World Water Forums

At the Third World Water Forum, in Kyoto, Japan, 2003, the Vatican, through its Pontifical Council for Justice and Peace (PCJP) noted the growing movement "to formally adopt a human right to water," founded on the basic dignity of the person. In this situation, the Vatican sees that linkages "between water policy and ethics increasingly emerge throughout the world."[25]

The 2004 *Compendium of the Social Doctrine of the Church* reiterates this view of the human right to water. With reference to John Paul II's 2004 address to the Brazilian Bishops' Conference stating that "everyone has a right to" water, the *Compendium* states that "satisfying the needs of all [for water], especially of those who live in poverty, must guide the use of water" (*Compendium* 484). In addition, "The right to water, as all human rights, finds its basis in human dignity and not in any kind of quantitative assessment that considers water as merely an economic good. Without water, life is threatened. Therefore the right to safe drinking water is a universal and inalienable right" (*Compendium* 485).[26]

In 2006, the PCJP delivered another important address at the Fourth World Water Forum in Mexico City. The statement notes the increasing recognition that access to safe water is "at the root of some of society's pressing concerns." Water is seen as an "essential, irreplaceable element to ensuring the continuance of life" and thus linked to fundamental rights such as the right to life.[27]

The PCJP declaration recognizes that all parties to international treaties have an "obligation to ensure that the minimum essential level of any right is realized; in this case of the right to water, which is considered to mean non-discriminatory access to enough water to prevent dehydration and disease." The statement is clear that access to clear and drinkable water is a "legal entitlement," not just a service or commodity provided on a humanitarian basis. At the same time, the declaration speaks of the need to recapture a "culture of water," and "to educate society to a new attitude towards water." The "action of wasting water is morally unsustainable." People in some countries

25. Pontifical Council for Justice and Peace, "Water, An Essential Element for Life," Vatican City, March 22, 2003, *www.vatican.va/roman_curia/pontifical_councils /justpeace/documents/rc_pc_justpeace_doc_20030322_kyoto-water_en.html*.

26. Pontifical Council for Justice and Peace, *Compendium of The Social Doctrine of the Church* (Washington, DC: United States Conference of Catholic Bishops, 2004).

27. Pontifical Council for Justice and Peace, "Water, An Essential Element for Life: An Update," Vatican City, March 21, 2006, *http://www.vatican.va/roman_curia /pontifical_councils/justpeace/documents/rc_pc_justpeace_doc_20060322_mexico-water_en.html*.

take advantage of their privileged access to freshwater and waste this life force with little regard to the impact "on the lives of their brothers and sisters in the rest of the world."[28]

The PCJP declared that solutions for securing water as a basic right "should express a preferential love and consideration for the poor. It is for those that the water issue is crucial for life." The PCJP ended by stating, "The water issue is truly a right to life issue."[29] Thus, the PCJP is on record with a strong argument and declaration that finds full expression in the 2010 legal pronouncement of the United Nations and the moral support in the encyclicals of Popes Benedict XVI and Francis. The PCJP delivered similar statements at other World Water Forums and in its 2013 book, *Water: The Essential Element for Life*.[30]

Pope Benedict XVI, *Caritas in veritate* (*Charity in Truth*)

Benedict XVI had already argued for the inalienable right to water in a message to the 2008 International Exposition of Saragossa (Zaragoza), Spain, July 15.[31] His 2009 encyclical *Caritas in veritate* underscores the PCJP's statement. For Benedict XVI, "The right to food, like the right to water, has an important place within the pursuit of other rights, beginning with the fundamental right to life." Through education, a public conscience that considers "food and access to water as universal rights of all human beings, without distinction or discrimination" must be developed (*CV* 27).

---

28. Ibid.

29. Ibid.

30. Istanbul, Turkey, 2009; Marseilles, France, 2012. The 2012 statement praises the UN's 2010 declaration of a legal right to water and calls upon all nations to recognize "the duty of solidarity to the most vulnerable and future generations." See Pontifical Council for Justice and Peace, "Water, An Essential Element for Life: Designing Sustainable Solutions, An Update," Marseilles, 2012 (Vatican City, 2013), *www.pcgp.it/dati/2012-03/09* and *www.iustitiaetpax.va/content/giustiziae pace/en/archivio/pubblicazioni/_water-an-essential-element-for-life--vatican-city -2013--pp--117.html*.

31. Benedict XVI, "Water: An Essential Good Given by God to Maintain Life," Letter to Cardinal Martino, International Expo at Zaragoza, July 15, 2008, *www .catholicculture.org/culture/library/view.cfm?recnum=8628*.

Pope Francis, *Laudato si'*:
On Care for Our Common Home

It falls to Francis in *Laudato si'* to underline again the importance of viewing access to freshwater as a universal human right. Francis's immediate concern is climate change, which he notes will impact "the availability of essential resources like drinking water" (*LS* 24). He argues strongly for access to fresh drinking water, not just for human life but also for all life on land and sea. In many places around the globe, demand exceeds sustainable supply, with shortages and poor management of supply common.

As noted in chapter 6, "Selling Water: Privatization of a Scarce Resource," access to water in a time of water scarcity is critical when it comes to the poor who daily suffer from unsafe water, leading to disease and death, particularly in the case of infants (*LS* 29). Francis argues that "[a]ccess to safe drinkable water is a basic and universal human right, since it is essential to human survival. Our world has a grave social debt towards the poor who lack access to drinking water, because they are denied the right to a life consistent with their inalienable dignity" (*LS* 30). He continues, "This indisputable fact overrides any other assessment of environmental impact on a region" (*LS* 164, 185).

Francis advances the argument of a right to water in several ways. First, he extends the indispensability of freshwater, free from pollution, to all life—human, animal, plant—on Earth. Second, he reinforces the 2010 UN declaration that water is a human right, setting a right to water as the foundation of the right to life with a corresponding obligation for authorities to ensure the exercise of that right. Third, Francis emphasizes the special needs of the poor and the debt they are owed in relation to water access. Other key principles involve a right to life itself, the stewardship of the goods of creation, the common good and not just the good of those who can afford privatized water, solidarity with poor people in their struggles for freshwater, and finally, the "inalienable dignity" of the poor, a dignity threatened by the inability to exercise their fundamental right to water.

Then in 2017 at an international seminar on the human right to water, sponsored by the Vatican's Pontifical Academy of Sciences,

Francis warned that the world could be moving toward "a major world war for water. . . . I ask if in this piecemeal third world war that we are living through, are we not going toward a great world war for water?" Francis spoke of "the urgent need" to address this issue because "all people have a right to safe drinking water," but the right is not guaranteed today.[32]

US Conference of Catholic Bishops

The US Conference of Catholic Bishops has issued several documents that relate to clean water. Though not expressing a human right to water, the statements imply that such a right exists.[33] Catholic Relief Services (CRS) has developed a statement on the right to water and has been active in advancing clean water projects. Catholic Rural Life, a national Catholic organization dedicated to the enhancement of rural living, has also worked on the right to water and water as an integral dimension of faith, in policies and activities.[34]

Implementation of a Human Right to Water: Case Study

After the 2010 UN declaration related to the implementation of a human right to water this concern arose: how does a state, or even a town or city, fulfill its obligation to meet that claim? South Africa has developed an encouraging example. Its 1998 National Water Act incorporates the principle of water as a "public trust" into the concept of a reserve, which requires a nonnegotiable distribution of water to meet needs for drinking, cooking, sanitation, and other basic uses.

---

32. Gerald O'Connell, "Pope Francis Warns of a 'Major World War for Water,'" *America*, February 24, 2017, *www.americamagazine.org/faith/2017/02/24/pope-francis-warns-major-world-war-water*.

33. See USCCB, "Renewing the Earth," 1991; "Global Climate Change: A Plea for Dialogue, Prudence, and the Common Good," 2001; "A Place at the Table," 2002, at *www.usccb.org*.

34. Catholic Relief Services, "Education," 2015, *www.crs.org*; Jason Gehrig, "Water and Conflict," October 2008, *www.crs.org/sites/default/files/tools-research/water-and-conflict.pdf*; Catholic Rural Life, "Education," *www.catholicrurallife/resources/education*.

The act also underscores water ecosystem protection as fundamental to the nation's water allocations, "so that the human use of water does not compromise the long term sustainability of aquatic and associated ecosystems."[35] Only after these two facets of the reserve have been safeguarded do other water uses, such as irrigation and industrial use, gain consideration.[36]

The South African approach includes active participation by residents within any given water basin. In this way, water withdrawals for agriculture and industry, for example, are balanced against ecological impacts of water lost to those uses. When water is protected as a basic right and is coupled with reserve policies and guidelines, principles of subsidiarity, solidarity, and participation show great promise for a "new water ethic." Recently, in the United States, the states of Hawaii, Connecticut, and Michigan appropriated forms of public trust doctrine to ensure water protection of entire ecosystems. Significantly, when human water rights conflict with public trust for ecosystem protection, public trust principles supersede water rights.[37]

Conclusion: A New Water Ethic

Recall Maude Barlow's words at the beginning of this chapter: "If we can determine that water is a right, it gives citizens a tool they can use against their governments."[38] In a similar vein, Sandra Postel, director of the Global Water Policy Project, calls for an international convention on water. She underscores that "the ethical dimensions of society's water use and management choices" must be an integral part of water policies in a new water ethic. "Our moral obligations both to our fellow human beings and to other life-forms implore us to manage water as the basis of life for all living things, rather than as a commodity for the benefit of some."[39]

---

35. Quoted in Postel and Richter, *Rivers for Life*, 84–85.

36. Ibid., 86.

37. Ibid., 108.

38. Maude Barlow, senior adviser on water issues to the president of the UN General Assembly, quoted in Schleifer, "Is Access to Clean Water a Basic Human Right?" *Christian Science Monitor, http://www.csmonitor.com/2009/0319/p06s01-woeu.html.*

39. Postel and Richter, *Rivers for Life*, 118.

In relation to a right to water for all Earth as Francis emphasizes, along with the legal basis laid out in the 2010 UN declaration, a human right to water is firmly established. CST adds key emphases upon serving the common good in global solidarity with local participation and rooted in a preferential option for the poor, which requires that those with more share—even possibly surrendering their own right to water. A new water ethic is now in place, one that can be called upon to guide policies and practices in coming years. Chapter 8, "A New Water Ethic: Because Water Is Life," explores what some of those policies and practices might involve, as well as the possibility of expanding CST to include the natural world's right to water.

Review Questions

1. What is a "right"?
2. What arguments support the 2010 UN declaration that there is a human right to water?
3. What arguments does CST use to support a human right to water?
4. What does CST add to the UN's declaration to prove a right to water?
5. What major principles does CST use to support a right to water?

Discussion Questions

1. What are some possible reasons why the United States did not sign the 2010 UN declaration?
2. What arguments would you use to convince your congressional representatives to urge the United States to sign the declaration? Explain.
3. Which of CST's arguments for a right to water do you find most convincing? Why?
4. What difference do the teachings of Christianity make in arguing for a universal right to water?

A New Water Ethic
Because Water Is Life

America needs nothing less than a revolution in how we use water. This revolution will bring about the ethical use of water in every sector. Such an ethic is as essential as past awakenings to threats against our environment and ourselves: the way we stopped tossing litter out car windows and trashing public parks. . . . Perhaps . . . I could find some common ground for a water ethic in the Bible and other religious texts.

—*Cynthia Barnett, journalist*[1]

"Water is life." That has been the main theme throughout these discussions. In the course of developing an ethical framework to examine the global water crises, this text has examined water through the lens of Catholic social teaching (CST) since Pope Leo XIII's 1891 encyclical *Rerum novarum*, which literally means "of new things."[2] This final chapter looks at new technological developments related to the global water crises, but more importantly to new dimensions in the ethical and spiritual dimensions of water, so central to a response in action and thought. The first part of this chapter focuses on examples of possible and promising technological

---

1. Cynthia Barnett, *Blue Revolution*, 7, 146.

2. The pope uses the phrase "of new things" in *Rerum novarum* to refer to new revolutionary movements of the day.

solutions to various water crises. However, even though important and helpful in meeting these crises, these are not sufficient. A new water ethic and a sense of the spirituality surrounding water as a key, even basic, dimension of creation must serve as the basis for guiding policy and practice.

So, the second part of the discussion then involves new understandings regarding the natural world and water, as well as an expansion of Catholic social teaching to include the moral and legal rights of water and the belief that water is a sacred revelation of the divine presence in creation.

Part I: Water Policies and Practices

Although there are no definitive answers to the world's water crises, what follows indicates the tremendous efforts underway to protect and restore Earth's water, essential to all life.

Cleaning Water

As most campers know, drinking water from a spring is a little chancy, so they bring along a water filter, available at most sports and camping stores. However, these devices are more expensive than most people in the developing world can afford, ranging from $19 to $109 (Amazon.com). So, what are some less costly alternatives?

One such device involves nothing more than pouring polluted water into a vat filled with sand with a spigot at the bottom; the sand filters the contaminants, and clear water flows out the spigot. Another is an inexpensive nine-inch Lifestraw, a plastic tube with fine mesh filters that a person can use to suck water from questionable sources.[3] Another device cleans water with an ultraviolet purifier that removes impurities and uses sunlight to remove germs.[4]

---

3. Donald G. McNeil, "A $3 Water Purifier That Could Save Lives," *New York Times*, October 10, 2006, 20, *www.nytimes.com/2006/10/10/science*; Jennie Yabroff, "Water for the World," *Newsweek*, June 18, 2007, 20.

4. "A Glimpse of Light in the Distance," *Newsweek*, November 12, 2007, 12. There are several other promising variations on filtering systems using sand as a filter; see the BioSand Filter, for example. See also Freeman and Gower, "Big Gulp," 113.

Desalination

Desalination draws freshwater from salt water. In 2016, there were about 7,500 desalination plants in operation—two-thirds in the Middle East. Israel, for example, meets about one-third of its water needs through desalination.[5] The city of Brownsville, Texas, uses desalination and purifies brackish water to provide about one-fourth of its demand.[6]

Still problems remain. Desalination requires enormous energy, burns fossil fuels, and releases excessive greenhouse gases, is costly, and often releases salt waste, containing chemicals, into the sea, which can threaten the ocean's diversity.[7]

Dew Collecting, Fog Harvesting

Another approach to getting freshwater focuses on collecting it from the atmosphere. Dew collecting works on high hills when water from low clouds and fog collects in artificial ponds. In southern England, dew ponds dot the landscape.[8]

With fog-catching screens, large plastic sheets of mesh are erected to capture moisture from fog in places where there is little rain. Tiny droplets form larger drops on the mesh and run into troughs. For example, this approach is used at the edge of the Sahara Desert in Morocco.[9] Other new technologies to produce clean water are developing rapidly.

---

5. "Water in the West Bank," *Economist*, June 30, 2016, 38.

6. Lynn Berzosky, "Texas Begins Desalinating Sea Water," *Seattle Post-Intelligencer*, June 2, 2007. *https://usatoday30.usatoday.com/money/economy/2007-07-01-1129033506_x.htm*.

7. "The Impacts of Relying on Desalination for Water," *Scientific American* (n.d.), *www.scientificamerican.com/article/the-impacts-of-relying-on-desalination/*.

8. Pearce, *When the Rivers Run Dry*, 245–247; John Kitsteiner, "Dew Ponds or Dieu Ponds," *Temperate Climate Permacultaure*, July 8, 2011, *http://tcpermaculture.blogspot.com/2011/07/dew-ponds-or-dieu-ponds.html*; "Big Idea: A Well That Sucks Water from Air," *Time*, November 7, 2016, 17; Pearce, *When the Rivers Run Dry*, 261–65.

9. Jacopo Prisco, "Desert 'Fog Catchers' Make Water out of Thin Air," CNN Africa, November 18, 2016, *www.cnn.com/2016/11/18/africa/fog-catchers-morocco/*. For more suggestions, see: Pearce, *When the Rivers Run Dry*, 251–52.

Using Water More Efficiently: Agriculture, Industry, and Consumer Demand

Agriculture: Rainwater Harvesting and Drip Irrigation

Whether catching water in large vats, diverting flash floods to collection ponds or channels, putting small dams across streams to check the water, erecting earth dams in the desert, capturing flood-waters in wadis, or gullies, rainwater harvesting techniques are now spreading to parts of the world as diverse as Japan, Bangladesh, Pakistan, and Singapore.[10] In October 2008, Tucson, Arizona, for example, became the first US city to require all commercial developments to harvest rainwater.[11]

Simply put, rainwater harvesting involves collecting rain from rooftops or other high areas, storing the water in buckets, vats, or barrels, and then using it as needed for plants and crops, whether in backyard gardens in the United States or on farms in India. These schemes mean more water for village wells, higher-yielding crops, and year-round grain farming.[12] In this way, water issues are directly tied to poverty relief.

Drip irrigation, invented and patented by Simcha Blass in 1959, delivers water directly to plant roots using valves, pipes, or tubing, either above or below ground. Israel's agricultural success in its arid land is due entirely to drip irrigation.[13] By delivering water directly to plant roots, this method can reduce water use by 39–70 percent while doubling and tripling water efficiency in nurturing plants and crops, as compared with conventional methods used today.[14]

---

10. See Pearce, *When the Rivers Run Dry*, 267–71, for a fuller discussion of different technologies in a variety of cultures.

11. Jonathan Thompson, "Desperate Measures: Off the Roof," *High Country News*, November 24, 2008, 19.

12. Pearce, *When the Rivers Run Dry*, 262–65.

13. De Villiers, *Water*, 298–99.

14. Sandra Postel, *Liquid Assets: The Critical Need to Safeguard Freshwater Ecosystems* (Washington, DC: Worldwatch Institute, 2005), 40.

Industry: Lower Water Use, Reuse of Wastewater

Industry has made great progress in water use.[15] Factories in the industrialized world generally return more than 90 percent of the water they use from rivers,[16] although polluted and warmer water is sometimes the result.

In addition, several water-reuse projects are based on the premise that wastewater can be used for many purposes, such as flushing toilets and watering plants and crops. Denmark reuses 98 percent of its wastewater after treatment for such purposes.[17] Cloudcroft, New Mexico, was one of the first cities in the United States in which wastewater was treated and reused for drinking water; the city started its long-term project in 2004.[18]

Consumer Demand

Americans consume a lot of water directly and indirectly through the foods we eat. In 2016 the average daily water consumption per person in the United States was between 80 and 110 gallons for drinking, flushing, and bathing, direct uses.[19] That figure does not include indirect uses such as the 500 gallons needed to produce one pound of chicken or the 1,840 gallons needed for one pound of beef. Add the 350 gallons required for a half-pound of cheese. With those calculations in mind, Sarah Scoles, freelance science writer, calculated that in 2016, the average American consumed and used 2,088 gallons per day, which adds up to an astonishing US total of 664 billion gallons per day.[20]

Water-thirsty lawns are America's largest "crop," and efforts to reduce the acreage devoted to lawns are now advancing across the

---

15. De Villiers, *Water*, 298.

16. Robert Kandel, *Water from Heaven: The Story of Water from the Big Bang to the Rise of Civilization and Beyond* (New York: Columbia University Press, 2003), 257.

17. Kandel, *Water from Heaven*, 211, 255; Phillip Ball, *Life's Matrix: A Biography of Water* (New York: Farrar, Straus and Giroux, 1999), 356.

18. Peter Friederici, "Facing the Yuck Factor," *High Country News*, September 17, 2007, 8, 11; "Pioneering Water Reuse in the Old West," Waste and Wastewater International, *waterworld.com/articles/wwi/print,volume-24/issue-2/editorial-focus/pioneering -water-reuse-in-the-old-west.html*.

19. "How Much Water Does the Average Person Use at Home Per Day?" US Geological Survey, December 2, 2016, *water.usgs.gov/edu/qa-home-percapita.html*.

20. Sarah Scoles, "Parched," *Popular Science*, March–April 2017, 60.

country. "Xeriscaping," or landscaping that requires little or no irrigation, saves water by using low-water plants, mulching, efficient irrigation, and limited turf areas.[21] The amount of water saved can be dramatic: a study conducted by the Las Vegas Water Authority over several years found that in 2006 "where Xeriscaping replaced turf, water use dropped an average of 80%."[22]

Beyond agricultural, industrial, and government efforts, what can individuals do to reuse and consume less water? There are many possibilities, including the following:

- Limit or stop lawn watering.
- Eliminate baths and take "navy showers"—wetting down, turning off the water while lathering, and then rinsing off.
- Use low-flow or dual-flush toilets.[23]
- Use high-tech, water-efficient showerheads.
- Buy water-efficient clothes washers and dishwashers.
- Turn off the faucet while brushing teeth, combing hair, and more.
- Install drip irrigation for watering plants.
- Use xeriscaping and remove lawn.
- Build garden soil that is naturally healthy by using mulch and organic compost, growing native plants, limiting digging only to planting, and minimizing or eliminating use of pesticides, herbicides, and synthetic fertilizers.
- Wash cars only at sites that recycle water.
- Sweep sidewalks and patios instead of hosing them down.
- Wash full loads of laundry and dishes.[24]

---

21. Xeriscaping was first adopted by the Denver Water Department in 1981. See ROL Staff, "How to Have a Vibrant Garden without Using Lots of Water," *Rodales Organic Life*, October 4, 2017, *www.rodalesorganiclife.com/garden/how-have -vibrant-garden-without-wasting-water*.

22. Michelle Nijhuis, "The Lure of the Lawn," *High Country News*, 13.

23. Postel, *Liquid Assets*, 40. In the United States, water-efficient toilets, dishwashers, clothes washers, urinals, faucets, and showerheads, are estimated to save enough water per year to supply four to six times the population of New York City.

24. These are only a few suggestions; check with a local public utilities site for more information. Seattle Public Utilities, for example, has several useful suggestions: *www.seattle.gov/util/MyServices/Water/Reduce_Water_Use/index.htm*.

People can make food choices with water use in mind. For example, eating lower on the food chain and encouraging others to do so or moving from beef and pork to chicken or even going vegetarian will help save water. Clothing choices also matter. Cotton, for example, is a thirsty crop. Adopting habits that save water requires mindfulness of the value of water and its sacred nature.

Part II: CST—A New Water Ethic and an Ecological Spirituality

In *Laudato si': On Care for Our Common Home*, Pope Francis confronts human consumption,[25] particularly of energy, calling for wide-ranging lifestyle changes to lessen or help reverse climate change (*LS* 22, 23). He writes, "the present level of consumption in developed countries and wealthier sectors of society, where the habit of wasting and discarding has reached unprecedented levels," is not sustainable (*LS* 27). Although ecological sensitivity is growing around the world—something to be thankful for—it has not dampened people's "harmful habits of consumption which appear to be growing all the more" (*LS* 55). He cites the example of the increasing use of air conditioners (*LS* 55).

Francis then refers to reducing water consumption as a means of expressing environmental responsibility (*LS* 211). His final appeal to the Christian community is for a spirituality "capable of deep enjoyment free of the obsession with consumption." In addition, he challenges the "constant flood of new consumer goods," stating that "Christian spirituality proposes a growth marked by moderation and the capacity to be happy with little" (*LS* 222).

A New Water Ethic: A Call for New Water Management Policies

In 2006, the second UN World Water Development Report, *Water: A Shared Responsibility*, argued for "demand management," namely

---

25. In *Laudato si'*, Francis uses the word *consumption* thirty times, far more than his predecessors.

"using water more efficiently, and fairly, improving the balance between present supplies and demand, and reducing excessive use."[26]

Sandra Postel, Director, Global Water Policy Project, suggests several features of management principles useful in a new water ethic. First, humans must more fully adapt to nature's cycles by restoring free-flowing rivers and adjusting to droughts rather than attempting to control flows. Second, humans can reduce pressure on freshwater systems by reducing populations and consumption. In addition, people must increase water productivity by using drip irrigation; replacing water-thirsty crops with low-water-use ones; using agricultural and landscaping practices that build healthy, drought-resistant soils; shifting from animal to vegetable proteins in diets; and in the name of the common good, challenging the commodification and privatization of water. Finally, managers must fully use the "precautionary principle," that is, "err on the side of allocating too much water to ecosystems rather than too little."[27]

One avenue to better water management and to serving poor populations lies in modifying systems of social tariffs in which rich and poor pay different prices for drinking water and sanitation services and consumption levels are priced differently.[28] However, there is a need to go beyond management principles, as important as these are, to developing a new water ethic and to examining developments regarding the rights of nature and, consequently, the rights of water.

Earth Rights: Legal and Moral Consideration

The establishment of rights of nature is an exciting development in the study of ethics and shows that ethics is not static but expands. *Rights* in this context means that nature, including water, has legal

---

26. World Water Assessment Programme (United Nations), *Water: A Shared Responsibility*, the United Nations World Water Development Report 2 (New York: Berghahn Books, 2006), 7–8, 16, 19, 28.

27. Postel and Richter, *Rivers for Life*, 202–4.

28. Luis Fernando Yavari, "Management of Basic Drinking Water and Sanitation Services by a Cooperative in Bolivia," in *Reclaiming Public Water* (Amsterdam: Transnational Institute and Corporation, Europe Observatory, 2005), 39; Helio Maltz, "Porto Alegre's Water: Public and for All," *Reclaiming Public Water* (Amsterdam: Transnational Institute and Corporation, Europe Observatory, 2005), 32.

and moral rights and can make claims. The extension of rights to previously excluded groups, such as African Americans, women, indigenous peoples, and species (under the US Endangered Species Act), are examples of the continual extension of the concept of rights.

Postel highlighted this theme in referring to a 1972 dissent by William O. Douglas, associate justice of the US Supreme Court, in the case of *Sierra Club v. Morton*.[29] Douglas wrote, "[C]ontemporary public concern should lead to the conferral of standing upon environmental objects to sue for their own preservation." Douglas argued explicitly for rivers as plaintiffs: "The river as plaintiff speaks for the ecological unit of life that is part of it." Postel notes that legal scholar Christopher D. Stone "argued more than 35 years ago that yes, rivers and trees and other objects of nature do have rights, and these should be protected by granting legal standing to guardians of the voiceless entities of nature."[30]

Douglas's dissent and Stone's argument on the rights of nature were supported in Cochabamba, Bolivia, on Earth Day in 2010, when Maude Barlow, National Chairperson of the Council of Canadians, along with Vandana Shiva, an environmental leader from India, and other representatives drew up a Declaration of the Rights of Mother Earth: "the earth has a right 'to regenerate its bio-capacity and to continue its vital cycles and processes free from human disruptions.'"[31]

Postel's hope is that in extending rights to water, "it may well be that a new ethic will emerge, one that says it is not only right and good but necessary that all living things get enough water before some get more than enough."[32]

---

29. *Sierra Club v. Morton* pitted the environmental group against Disney Corporation, which was trying to build a ski resort in the Mineral King Valley in Sequoia National Forest. Disney received a permit from the US Forest Service to lease the property for thirty years. The Sierra Club objected to the construction. The Supreme Court ruled the club did not have legal standing. Justice Douglas wrote a strong dissenting opinion; Jonathan Zasloff, "The Mystery of *Sierra Club v. Morton*," *Legal Planet*, April 24, 2011, *http://legal-planet.org/2011/04/24/the-mystery-of-sierra-club-v-morton/*.

30. Sandra Postel, "The Missing Piece: A Water Ethic," in Brown and Schmidt, *Water Ethics*, 223.

31. Quoted in Jeremy J. Schmidt and Christiana Z. Peppard, "Water Ethics on a Human-Dominated Planet," *WIREs Water*, September 15, 2014, 16–17, *http://wires.wiley.com/WileyCDA/WiresJournal/wisId-WAT2.html DOI:wo.1002/wat2.1043*.

32. Postel, *Liquid Assets*, 223–24. See also Cormac Cullinan, "If Nature Had Rights" *Earth Letter*, Winter 2008–2009, 8–9 (originally appeared in *Orion*, January–February 2008).

The Whanganui River, New Zealand's third-largest river, has been declared a legal person with rights to be respected that prevent people from blocking its flows.

In March 2017, the New Zealand legislature declared the Whanganui River, the country's third largest, a legal person, "an entity with rights," "in the sense that it can own property, incur debts, and petition the courts." The Maori, the aboriginal people of New Zealand, have a deep connection to the Whanganui, as voiced in their proverb "I am the river and the river is me." The law views the river as a living whole; two guardians are appointed to act for the river, one from the government and the other from the Maori community.

Days later, a court in India declared that two of the country's most sacred rivers, the Ganges and the Yamuna, have the legal standing of persons. Referring to the Whanganui decision, the court assigned legal parents to protect the rivers. The decision enables the two rivers to claim that polluting them is a crime that harms not only people who enter the rivers but also the rivers themselves.[33]

A week later, the Uttarakhand High Court of India declared that "glaciers, rivers, streams, rivulets, lakes, air, meadows, dales, jungles, forests, wetlands, grasslands, springs and waterfalls" are legal/

---

33. "Try Me a River," *Economist*, March 25, 2017, 34.

juristic persons. A "juristic person," just like a natural person, has legal rights and obligations. Importantly, "The rights of these entities shall be equivalent to the rights of human beings and the injury/harm caused to these bodies shall be treated as harm/injury caused to the human beings."[34]

In the United States, in 2017, the Community Environmental Legal Defense Fund (CELDF) filed a lawsuit against Colorado's governor. The suit asks that the Colorado River be recognized as a legal person with rights "of its own to exist and flourish." CELDF is seeking a ruling that the river and its ecosystem "possess certain rights, including the right to exist, flourish, evolve, regenerate, and restoration." In support of the arguments, the CELDF cited Douglas's 1972 dissent.[35] These legal decisions provide an important basis for expanding CST to include the rights to health, integrity, and preservation for nature and water.

New Water Ethic: Catholic Environmental and Social Teachings

The model of an ecologically sound Christianity requires the extension of rights to all parts of an ecosystem, including water, not only because of each part's contribution to the whole but also because each part is a strand in the web of creation and has inherent, intrinsic worth.

Pope Francis states this clearly in *Laudato si'*: "By virtue of our unique dignity and our gift of intelligence, we are called to respect creation and its inherent laws, for 'the Lord by wisdom founded the earth'" (Prv 3:19; *LS* 69). Francis argues at length for the rights of humans, including a human right to water. Now, this chapter will look at arguments extending the already examined principles of CST to include the rights of water itself. Note that when the rights of water conflict with other rights, including basic rights of humans, water's rights may be overridden, but such an overruling demands

---

34. "Uttarakhand HC Declares Air, Glaciers, Forests, Springs, Waterfalls, Etc. as Legal Persons," *Live Law*, April 1, 2017, *www.livelaw.in/uttarakhand-hc-declares-air-glaciers-forests-springs-waterfalls-etc-legal-persons/*.

35. See "Rights of Nature: Overview," Community Environmental Legal Defense Fund, *https://celdf.org/rights/rights-of-nature/*.

fair adjudication. Though specifics are yet to be formulated, the basic principle remains and should find a place in a needed revision of CST that focuses on natural rights and the environment.

A New Ecological Ethic in CST

In a 2006 document, Maryknoll, a Catholic worldwide organization of priests, brothers, sisters, and lay missionaries, supported this ethical/theological framework, much in the spirit of Francis. In *Water and the Community of Life*, they wrote, "Water . . . claims its own 'right to be' by the very fact that it is! To honor water is to go deep into the very mystery of creation. . . . Water is an 'endangered species'; its purity, nurturing power, free-flow and availability for all under attack."[36]

The authors apply several major CST principles to water: "as we better understand the full implications of our being members of a single, sacred earth community, the common good must be expanded to include all other expressions of earth life. Therefore, our concern for the common good must reach out and incorporate the 'good' of water." Furthermore, the principle of participation must "ensure that the rights of the natural world are also represented at the table. . . . Our work with sister water moves us beyond social participation to include ecological participation."[37]

The insights of the Maryknoll document can expand to other CST principles in relation to water's rights, such as the basic right of water to flourish without diminution, pollution, or removal from the public commons of Earth. Other CST principles that relate to the rights of water are as follows:

- Equality demands that water be recognized as an integral part of the whole and treated well in balancing the goods of Earth.
- Following the hydrologic cycle, water has a basic right of association throughout its manifestations as rain, snow, ice, steam, and evaporation.

---

36. Maryknoll Office for Global Concerns, *Water and the Community of Life* (Washington, DC: 2006), 24–25, *www.maryknoll.org/globalconcerns*.

37. Ibid., 26–27.

- Water involves a preferential option where it is marginalized, impoverished, and polluted—calling for its restoration to integrity and wholeness.
- The obligations of water are to ensure life and the flourishing of other creatures and Earth.[38]

A Spirituality of Water

In *Laudato si'*, Francis speaks of the need for an ecological spirituality, because "spirituality can motivate us to a more passionate concern for the protection of our world" (*LS* 216). Jesuit Fr. Frank Turner writes that "[f]or Christians, water is both a necessarily fundamental ecological theme and also a spiritual symbol. . . . [I]t evokes Christ himself who refers to himself as 'living water' and it evokes ways of new life, as in the sacrament of Baptism."[39]

While the concept of *sacrament*[40] has often referred to the Catholic Church's seven sacraments,[41] the term *sacramental* has a broader meaning, namely, a way of saying that such a reality reveals the divine presence, a "breaking in" of the Divine in all of creation.

For Christians the Genesis story itself reveals the divine presence in water: "Now the earth was a formless void, there was darkness over the deep, and God's spirit hovered over the water" (Gen 1:2). In this Creation story, waters were the original stuff of the universe, present before the rest of the created world. All life emerges from the deep, possessed of the Spirit of God.

---

38. As Peter G. Brown notes, "In the commonwealth of life we find obligations that are human-to-nonhuman, if not consciously or enforceably the other way around as well." Peter Brown, "Are There Any Natural Resources?," in *Water Ethics*, ed. Brown and Schmidt, 214. See also Barlow and Clark, *Blue Gold*, 221, for a similar set of guiding principles concerning water.

39. Frank Turner, "Water in Catholic Social Teaching," *Ecojesuits: Ecology and Jesuits in Communication*, August 31, 2013, *www.ecojesuit.com/water-in-catholic-social-teaching/5691/*.

40. For further discussion in a Catholic context, see John Hart, "Nature's Natural Rights," *Sacramental Commons: Christian Ecological Ethics* (Lanham, MD: Rowman and Littlefield, 2006), 117–38.

41. These seven are Baptism, Confirmation, Eucharist, Reconciliation (Confession), Marriage, Ordination to the Priesthood, and Anointing of the Sick.

Other accounts of water in the tradition build upon its inherent sacred nature. The early Christian theologian Tertullian (c.155–240 CE), wrote that water is the first "seat of the divine Spirit . . . the first to produce what has life. . . . Therefore all natural water gains the power of sanctifying in the sacrament."[42] When Christianity arrived in areas of Europe, the powers associated with rivers, streams, and wells were recognized and "Christianized," named after a saint or the Virgin Mary. For example, the well waters at Chartres, St. Winifred's Well in Wales, Chalice Well of Glastonbury, and the "miraculous" spring at Lourdes, France, are regarded as sacred precisely because they produce miracles of healing. Even today, there are estimated to be some 3,000 holy wells in Ireland.[43] Churches and monasteries were built alongside streams and rivers, where the pagan Celts had worshiped a water goddess. The Cistercian monks followed Celtic customs in their regard for the sacredness of water, choosing lands near water temples.[44]

The biblical accounts of the life of Jesus are filled with references to the physical and spiritual powers of water. Jesus is baptized in the Jordan River and cures people at the pool of Bethesda in the temple (see Jn 5: 1–18). The Gospel states the power of water's symbolic, sacred meaning when Jesus merges water's cleansing powers and the powers to purify the spirit: "No one can enter the kingdom of God without being born of water and spirit" (Jn 3:5). Spirit infuses the waters, living signs of God's indwelling in the primal forces of the created world.

Rituals: Purification and Blessings

Catholic rituals also emphasize the material and spiritual purifying powers of water. Upon entering a church, one dips fingers into a holy-water font to purify and set aside the impurities of the outside world. At times the assembled congregation is sprinkled with water, meant to symbolize purification. Sprinkling water is used in

---

42. Quoted in Mircea Eliade, *Patterns in Comparative Religion* (New York: Sheed and Ward, 1958), 196–97.

43. McDonagh, *Dying for Water*, 99.

44. Nathaniel Altman, *Sacred Water: The Spiritual Source of Life* (Mahwah, NJ: Hidden Spring, 2000), 90, 114.

ceremonies to bless boats, houses, animals, and other possessions. Water is used in exorcism rituals to ward off evil manifestations, and finally, a burial coffin is sprinkled with water to prepare the deceased for the journey to the next world.[45]

Water as Sacred, Revealing Divine Presence

Theologian John Hart investigates the central connection between the material and the spiritual realities of water when he discusses water as sacrament.[46] He asks how if the waters are polluted or privatized, they can be "sacramental," that is, how can water embody the Divine? How can Spirit inhabit contaminated water or water that some have "stolen" from the community at large? For their own needs, some fail to treat water as a common good provided by the Creator for the benefit of all, humans, animals, plants, and Earth itself.

Hart writes, "Throughout the world today, environmental degradation and water privatization have caused water to lose its nature as a bountiful source of benefits needed to provide for the common good. Water is losing also its ability to be a sacramental symbol, a sign in nature of God the Creator." When Christians fully realize the intimate connection between the material and spiritual realities of water, only then will the Divine continue to be expressed in the world. If Christians see the water used in baptism and blessings as polluted, filled with contaminants, how will the reality of Baptism's promise of a new life be expressed?[47]

Back to Pope Francis

Many of the preceding reflections are exemplified in *Laudato si'*, in particular Francis's emphasis upon the intimacy involved in relations among humans, the natural world, and Earth. Although to many

---

45. For a further discussion of rituals and practices in the Catholic Church, see Chamberlain, *Troubled Waters*, 44–50.

46. Hart, "Living Water," *Sacramental Commons*, 33. He explains the sense in which creation is sacramental: "Creation is sacramental because it is the mediation of place of revelation of the immanent presence [presence in the ordinary, everyday world] of the Spirit."

47. Hart, "Living Water," *Sacramental Commons*, 70–96.

his language is only metaphorical, Francis emphasizes the new ways humans must express in their relationships with the created world. All creation is expressive of Spirit; each member of Earth community, "our common home," has intrinsic value for itself and not because of its usefulness to others.

Francis begins with a reference to Francis of Assisi's "Canticle of the Creatures," noting that Earth is "like a sister with whom we share our life and a beautiful mother who opens her arms to embrace us" (*LS* 1). He ends with a prayer noting the value of each element of creation:

> All-powerful God, you are present in the whole universe and in the smallest of your creatures. . . . Pour out upon us the power of your love, that we may protect life and beauty. Bring healing to our lives, that we may protect the world and not prey on it, that we may sow beauty, not pollution and destruction. (*LS* 246)

Between *Laudato si's* beginning and ending, Francis asks that "we feel *intimately* united with all that exists" (*LS* 11). He also states that "God is *intimately* present to each being, without impinging on the autonomy of his [*sic*] creature" (*LS* 80). An ecological spirituality is rooted in "the awareness that each creature reflects something of God and has a message to convey to us" (*LS* 221). He refers to the sixteenth-century mystic John of the Cross, who sensed "the *intimate* connection between God and all beings, and thus feels that 'all things are God'" (*LS* 234). Francis ends the encyclical with special reference to the Spirit: "Spirit, infinite bond of love, is *intimately* present at the very heart of the universe" (*LS* 238).

By using images of family (sister water, mother earth) and designating relationships as intimate, Francis formulates a new spirituality in which humans reconstitute relationships with Earth, not as one of domination or even stewardship but something much more powerful and so much more responsible on the part of humans for "the care of our common home." Our call, our vocation, as Christians, then, is to foster and develop this relationship of intimacy with Earth, and in particular with sister water. This new spirituality serves well as foundation for a new and more inclusive Catholic social and environmental ethic.

If people felt water were a sister, would they let her be disfigured, kept unclean (contaminated, polluted)? Would they let her be bought and sold, traded (privatization)? Would they not care for her health and well-being? Such is Francis's view: sister water is not a metaphor but forms a real and intimate relationship with us humans.

Conclusion

The new approaches to gain "more" water and use less are necessary but not sufficient. Rather, the water crises require fundamentally new understandings and valuations of water in a new water ethic. For this undertaking, recognition of water's rights can find expression in an expanded set of Catholic environmental and social teachings. Christiana Zenner (formerly Peppard) "wonders what it would take to prioritize, theologically, ethically, and institutionally, issues of fresh water access in the global church."[48] The expansion of CST to include water and water's rights in its basic principles begins to address her concern.

By caring for water, humans care not only for themselves but also for creation. The call is clear: all people should argue for the rights of water as an integral part of creation. Caring for water involves restraint over individual and collective use of water and ending the overconsumption of water, as well as greater advocacy for water policies and practices that impact human and nonhuman communities across Earth.

This discussion of CST and water began with Francis's encyclical on the environment, *Laudato si'*. It is fitting, then, to end with some of his final reflections, and with a fresh understanding of promising directions for CST, perhaps even a set of Catholic environmental and social teachings.

In concluding his encyclical, Francis asserts, "the ecological crisis is also a summons to profound interior conversion," a conversion that leads to an ecological spirituality, involving an intimate connection with Earth (*LS* 217). However, he cautions doctrine alone cannot ground this spirituality; inspiration to act and to change is also

---

48. Peppard, *Just Water*, 67.

needed: "More than in ideas or concepts as such, I am interested in how such a spirituality can motivate us to a more passionate concern for the protection of our world" (*LS* 216). Over the century, CST has developed from the rights of workers to the rights of all peoples and of Earth.

Review Questions

1. What are some ways to save water in agricultural uses? Which appear to be the most effective?
2. What are the promises and problems of desalination of seawater?
3. How can wastewater be used and reused?
4. Which CST documents are most helpful in promoting less water consumption? Why?
5. What are the key components of a new water ethic?

Discussion Questions

1. Is rainwater harvesting practiced in your area? If yes, by what means? If no, explore reasons why, including the possibility that the practice is illegal in your area.
2. Would you drink treated "wastewater"? Under what conditions?
3. What practical steps can you, as a consumer, take to consume less water?
4. If bottled water is used in one's family, workplace, or school, should one, based on principles of Catholic social teaching, implement a strategy to ban water bottles? Explain.
5. How would you argue for a new water ethic—a new approach for water's rights?

Additional Resources

Water
Books and Articles

Altman, Nathanial. *Sacred Water: The Spiritual Source of Life*. Mahwah, NJ: Hidden Spring, 2000. A look at the place of water in religious rituals.

Barlow, Maude. *Blue Covenant: The Global Water Crisis and the Coming Battle for the Right to Water*. New York: The New Press, 2007. A look over the struggles associated with privatization of water.

Barlow, Maude, and Tony Clarke. *Blue Gold: The Fight to Stop the Corporate Theft of the World's Water*. New York: The New Press, 2002. Excellent overview of water commodification, privatization.

Barnett, Cynthia. *Blue Revolution: Unmaking America's Water Crisis*. Boston: Beacon Press, 2011. Important discussion of the need for a new water ethic.

Brown, Peter, and Jeremy Schmidt, eds. *Water Ethics: Foundational Readings for Students and Professionals*. Washington State: Island Press, 2010. Essays cover historical development of water policies, from policies of dominion to a discussion of water's rights.

Chamberlain, Gary. *Troubled Waters: Religion, Ethics, and the Global Water Crises*. Lantham, MD: Rowman and Littlefield, 2008. Examination of indigenous, Western, and Eastern religious traditions surrounding water in relation to a new understanding of the sacred dimensions of water.

Fishman, Charles. *The Big Thirst: The Secret Life and Turbulent Future of Water*. New York: Free Press, 2011. Anecdotal discussions of water issues in several areas of the world, such as Australia, India and Las Vegas.

Glennon, Robert. *Unquenchable: America's Water Crisis and What To Do About It*. Washington: Island Press, 2009. Very readable coverage of current water crises in the United States with promising suggestions for solution.

Goodell, Jeff. *The Water Will Come: Rising Seas, Sinking Cities, and the Remaking of the Civilized World*. New York, NY: Little, Brown and Company, 2017. Discussion and analysis of climate change, especially rising sea levels, more powerful storms.

McDonald, Bernadette, and Douglas Jehl, eds. *Whose Water Is It? The Unquenchable Thirst of a Water-Hungry World.* Washington, DC: National Geographic, 2013.

Parker, Kathleen. "Clean Water Down the Toilet: More Than a Drop in the Bucket," *Seattle Times,* May 31, 2011, A 17. A look at using wastewater for flushing toilets.

Peppard, Christiana Z. *Just Water: Theology, Ethics, and the Global Water Crisis.* Maryknoll, NY: Orbis Press, 2014. An incisive look at several uses of water, such as agriculture, fracking, and a framework for a Christian response.

Shiva, Vandana. *Water Wars: Privatization, Pollution, and Profit.* Berkeley, CA: North Atlantic Books, 2016. Update to her 2002 classic with new introductions; still an incisive look at important issues.

UN World Water Development Report 4, vol. 1. Paris. UNESCO, 2012.

Water: Our Thirsty World. National Geographic, A Special Issue, April 2010.

Wile, Rob. "The American Lawn Is Now the Largest Single 'Crop' In The U.S.," *Huffington Post.* August 17, 2015, *www.huffingtonpost.com/entry /lawn-largest-crop-america_us_55d0dc06e4b07addcb43435d.*

Websites

Climate Reality Project, The, *www.climatereality.com.* A good general source for climate issues, and water.

CUESA: Cultivating a Healthy Food System, *http://www.cuesa.org/article /10-ways-farmers-are-saving-water.*

Foodtank: The Think Tank for Food, *https://foodtank.com/news/2013/03 /more-food-less-water-top-6-farming-practices-to-better-manage-water -use/.*

Michigan Water Stewardship Program, *www.miwaterstewardship.org/youth stewards/factsaboutwater/testyourknowledge/yourwaterconsumption.* Offers a quick way to check your water usage.

National Aeronautics and Science Administration, *www.nasa.gov/subject /3135/water.*

National Oceanic and Atmospheric Administration, *www.noaa.gov/ps:// -.*

Nature Conservancy, The, *https://support.nature.org/site/Advocacy?cmd =display&page=UserAction&id=140.*

Regeneration International, *http://regenerationinternational.org/why-regenerative -agriculture/.*

Saving Water Partnership, *www.savingwater.org/.* Offers practical examples of ways to save water.

"See Where Access to Clean Water Is Getting Better—and Worse," *National Geographic*, March 1, 2016, *www.nationalgeographic.com/clean -water-access-around-the-world/#select/TOT/total.*

Waste2Water: Partnership for a Cleaner Tomorrow, *www.Waste2water.com.* A good look at converting wastewater to drinking water.

Water Footprint Calculator: The Hidden Water in Everyday Products, *https://water.org/our-impact/water-crisis/.* Discusses global issues concerning water and offers a way to calculate one's water footprint.

Water Project, The, *https://thewaterproject.org/why-water/.*

Films

Entertaining Angels, directed by Michael Ray Rhodes, featuring Martin Sheen, Moira Kelly (1996). Follows early life of Dorothy Day, founding of the Catholic Worker movement.

Flow: For Love of Water, documentary featuring Vandana Shiva and Maude Barlow among others in an exploration of global water pollution and privatization around the world (2008), *www.youtube.com /watch?v=TvtnVQPxmzM.*

On the Waterfront, directed by Elia Kazan, featuring Marlon Brando, Karl Malden, Lee J. Cobb, Eva Marie Saint (1954). Film is based on work of Jesuit priest on union violence and corruption among longshoremen on the waterfronts of Hoboken, New Jersey.

From the Heart of the World, directed by Alan Ereia (1990), *www.youtube .com/watch?v=hRgTtrQOiRO.* Story of the Kogi, indigenous people of Colombia, whose beliefs center around water.

Troubled Water, PBS documentary, aired October 17, 2017. A documentary on coal ash: Duke Energy denials.

Troubled Waters, produced and directed by Terry D. Peterson, Jean Robinson, and narrated by Lynn Redgrave (2006; Interfaith Broadcasting Commission), *www.uccresources.com/products/troubled-waters-clean-water-global -issue-dvd.* A powerful review of water crises around the world.

Troubled Waters, produced by Claire Caulfield et al., filmed on Vancouver Island, British Columbia, Canada (2017; A News21 Production). *https:// troubledwater.news21.com/documentary/*; from the BBC: *www.you tube.com/watch?v=YACTNvuijQY*; *www.indiegogo.com/projects/troubled -water-documentary-film#/.*

Catholic Social Teachings
Books and articles

Bergman, Roger. *Catholic Social Learning: Educating the Faith That Does Justice*. New York: Fordham University Press, 2011. A discussion of how to educate for social justice.

Coleman, John, ed. *One Hundred Years of Catholic Social Thought*. Maryknoll, NY: Orbis Books, 1991. Series of articles on the history of CST, the family, work, and peace issues in CST.

DeBerri, Edward, and James Hug. *Catholic Social Teaching: Our Best Kept Secret*, 4th ed. Maryknoll, NY: Orbis Books, 2005. Updated version of a quick guide to CST, with summaries of papal and regional conference documents.

Dorr, Donal. *Option for the Poor and for the Earth: Catholic Social Teaching*. Maryknoll, NY: Orbis Books, 2012. An update of Dorr's earlier classic, *Option for the Poor*, looks at the strengths and weaknesses of CST.

Hart, John. *Sacramental Commons: Christian Ecological Ethics*. Lanham, MD: Rowman and Littlefield, 2006. A well-developed discussion of a new vision and spirituality of the world grounded in a Catholic sensibility for the divine presence in all Creation.

Himes, Kenneth, ed. *Modern Catholic Social Teaching: Commentaries and Interpretations*. Washington, D.C.: Georgetown University Press, 2004. Chapter 1 gives an especially fine discussion of the biblical roots of CST; commentaries on the major papal encyclicals on CST up to *Centessimus annus* in 1991.

Himes, Kenneth. *Responses to 101 Questions on Catholic Social Teaching*. New York: Paulist Press, 2001. A short book of brief responses to questions about CST on an everyday level.

Massaro, Thomas. *Living Justice: Catholic Social Teaching in Action*. Lanham, MY: Rowman and Littlefield, 2008.

McCarthy, David, ed. *The Heart of Catholic Social Teaching: Its Origins and Contemporary Significance*. Grand Rapids, MI: Brazos Press, 2009. An introduction to Catholic social teaching that includes exploration of practices, liturgies, and theologies supporting CST historically.

Mich, Marvin H. *Catholic Social Teaching and Movements*. Mystic, CT: Twenty-Third Publications, 1998. Excellent discussion of the context and implications of CST.

O'Brien, David, and Thomas Shannon. *Catholic Social Teaching: The Documentary Heritage*. 3rd rev. ed. Maryknoll, NY: Orbis Books, 2016. Complete documents on CST from 1891 to Pope Francis's recent *Laudato si* (2015). The "bible" for readers on CST documents.

Pontifical Council for Justice and Peace. *Compendium of the Social Doctrine of the Church.* Washington, DC: US Conference of Catholic Bishops, 2004. *www.vatican.va/roman_curia/pontifical_councils/justpeace/documents /rc_pc_justpeace_doc_20060526_compendio-dott-soc_en.html.* A systematic discussion of CST by topics; a basic resource for discussion of CST.

Sniegocki, John. *Catholic Social Teaching and Economic Globalization.* Milwaukee, WI: Marquette University Press, 2009. An interdisciplinary study of the negative effects of globalization and possible alternatives, using CST as an ethical guide.

Sullins, Paul, and Anthony Blasi, eds. *Catholic Social Thought: American Reflections on the Compendium.* Lanham, MD: Rowman and Littlefield, 2009.

Websites

Catholic Climate Covenant. *www.catholicclimatecovenant.org.* Overall view of the Catholic Church's role on climate change.

Creation Justice Ministries, *www.creationjustice.org.*

International Jesuit Ecology Project, Healing Earth: Water. *www.Healing earth.ijep.net/water.* Very good resource on presentations; statements on water; the site as a whole covers major environmental issues.

Papal Documents: Holy See. *www.vatican.va/offices/papal_docs_list.html.* Major Church documents on environmental and social issues.

St. Paul-Minneapolis Social Justice Center. *www.cctwincities.org/education -advocacy/catholic-social-teaching/.* Excellent resource for all documents on CST, mainly papal and US Conference of Catholic Bishops; complete with document references for particular words, phrases, and ideas. Like a dictionary on CST.

Organizations

Catholic Relief Services (CRS). *www.crs.org/.* Works around the world on immigration, refugees, and water issues; provides for many projects on water.

Catholic Rural Life. *https://catholicrurallife.org/.* Dedicated to service rural areas of the United States on water, agriculture, and justice issues.

Interfaith Center on Corporate Responsibility. *www.iccr.org/.* National coalition of three hundred religious institutional investors working to achieve a social and environmental return on investments.

Northwest Coalition for Responsible Investment, NWCRI. *https://issuu .com/ipjc/docs/nwcri_annual_report_2014.* Twenty-three-year-old Catholic organization dedicated to environmental and social justice issues.

Index

Note: The abbreviations, *c, i, s,* or *n* that follow page numbers indicate charts, illustrations, sidebars or footnotes, respectively.